LEADING SCHOOLS LEGALLY

The ABCs of School Law, Indiana Supplement

Third Edition

LEADING SCHOOLS LEGALLY

The ABCs of School Law, Indiana Supplement

Third Edition

David Emmert

POWER PUBLISHING

Leading Schools Legally
The ABCs of Indiana School Law

David Emmert

© 2005, 2008, 2011 by Power Publishing
All rights reserved. Published 2011.
First edition published 2005. Second edition 2008.
Printed in the United States of America.

ISBN-13: 9780979589928
ISBN-10: 0979589924

Library of Congress Control Number: 2008939089

Power Publishing
13680 N. Duncan Drive
Camby, IN 46113
(317) 347-1051
www.powerpublishinginc.com

Cover and interior design: Parada Design

FOREWORD

Leading Schools Legally—The ABCs of Indiana School Law has three main purposes. First, it provides a thorough overview of the Indiana Collective Bargaining Law, as amended in 2011. Second, it supplements the book, *Leading Schools Legally—A Practical Anthology of School Law,* second edition, 2008, by addressing Indiana and federal statutory and case law that was too voluminous to include in the book. Third, it is a quick but substantive reference to assist administrators in the everyday leadership of a school or school corporation.

Nothing in this book should be construed as legal advice. Consultation with the school attorney who is trained to apply the law to a particular set of facts is necessary for a proper resolution of a specific matter. This material is designed to be a guide for administrators, board members, attorneys, and students of school law when first considering an existing or potential legal issue.

CONTENTS

ARTICLE I: COLLECTIVE BARGAINING IN INDIANA PUBLIC SCHOOLS

ARTICLE II: ABCs OF SCHOOL LAW

A

B

C

D

E

F

ARTICLE I

Collective Bargaining In Indiana Public Schools

I. The Right to Bargain Collectively

Indiana's public employees have no common law (court-created) right to engage in collective bargaining with their government employers. Although there is a constitutional right to organize and speak for the improvement of wages and working conditions, the only right to bargain or negotiate with a government employer must be granted by the state Legislature for a statewide group, or by specific local governmental subdivisions such as cities, towns, counties, and school corporations. The only statewide group to be given this right is public school teachers who are employed by school corporations and charter schools.

Teachers, as a specific employee group, were given the right to collectively bargain in 1973 when the General Assembly passed the Certificated Educational Employee Bargaining Act ("CEEBA"). CEEBA was significantly amended by P.L. 48-2011 to (1) limit the subjects that must be bargained, (2) expand the required subjects of discussion, (3) compact the time period for reaching agreement, including a "last, best offer" final step (where a factfinder must select, in total, one or the other side's final offer), and (4) limit the maximum time period that a contract may exist to the end of each two year state budget biennium, the first being the period of July 1, 2011 through June 30, 2013.

Due to the constitutional doctrine of impairment of contract that prohibits legislative or executive alteration of any contract during its term of existence, numerous contracts will remain unaffected by P.L. 48's changes until their respective expiration dates (one of which is known to expire in 2018).

A. Voluntary Collective Bargaining with Non-Teacher Groups

Historically, some school boards across Indiana have chosen to recognize and bargain with agents selected by different groups of non-teacher employees such as bus drivers, secretaries, as well as maintenance and cafeteria staff. Once a group has been recognized by and negotiated with the school board, the resulting contract is enforceable during its term, but there is no legal requirement that it continue beyond its expiration date. Neither is there a state or federal agency that oversees or governs the relationship between the school and a non-teacher union. Only the courts, or an arbitrator if provided for in the contract, can resolve a contractual dispute. Thus, while a school board cannot abrogate a bargained contract during its term, it can refuse to bargain a new one.

School boards and administrators do need to be aware that non-teacher employees have the First Amendment right of speech and association which allows them to form and/or join a union, pay dues, elect officers, and *seek* official recognition and bargaining rights from school boards. Because no federal or state statue requires boards to recognize non-teacher unions, these groups may not use the judicial system to compel recognition and bargaining.

B. The Collective Bargaining Law "CEEBA"

With the enactment of "Public Law 217," or CEEBA, in 1973, the General Assembly authorized and required school corporations to collectively bargain with their teachers. A teacher covered by CEEBA's protection is technically termed a "school employee," which is referenced as a "certificated employee," the meaning being a person "(1) whose contract with the school corporation requires that the person hold a license or permit from the division of professional standards of the department under IC 20-28; or (2) who is employed as a teacher by a charter school established under IC 20-24." See IC 20-29-2.

Certificated school employees of a charter school established under IC 20-24 are expressly authorized to organize and bargain collectively, and enjoy the same rights as those employed in school corporations and educational cooperatives under CEEBA. (Teachers in a conversion charter school remain part of the unit of the sponsor school and are covered by the collective bargaining agreement in effect at that sponsoring school.)

The term "school corporation" as defined by CEEBA includes cooperatives involved with career and technical education, as well as those teaching children with disabilities. According to Indiana Education Employment Relations Board (hereinafter referenced as IEERB), there are presently 310 separate public school entities that bargain with their teacher groups (291 school corporations, 19 cooperatives, and no charters).

Note: The Indiana Code citation for CEEBA is IC 20-29, and includes nine chapters. Any Indiana Education Code reference may be found on the Internet at: www.in.gov/legislative/ic/code/title20. Either the appropriate "article number" (such as "29" for collective bargaining) may be selected, or if all four numbers of the Code are known (i.e., Title, Article, Chapter, Section, or "TACS"), each number may be inserted into the four boxes found on the lower right of this site:

T   A   C   S

II. Discretionary Collective Bargaining with Non-Teacher Groups

A. Process to Gain Recognition

Because there is no statutorily established legal mechanism for groups of non-teacher employees in a discretionary collective bargaining situation to select a bargaining agent, employees may initiate the process by such means as "card signing," petitioning, or conducting their own secret ballot vote to decide whether a particular bargaining agent should represent them.

The signing of a card is simply a means to gather evidence that a majority of the employees in a particular group desires to form a union organization to represent their interests with the goal of obtaining recognition and bargaining rights from the school board. The card will indicate signing employee authorizes a particular group or union to represent his or her interests in matters dealing with the board including collective bargaining. The card may also reveal that the employee has or will join the union as a dues paying member.

A school board has total discretion as to whether or not to recognize such a group, and even if the group is recognized, the board may or may not choose to bargain with it. Therefore, should less than fifty percent of the employees in that group indicate interest in such union, it would be unwise for the board to consider recognition of the group.

B. Recognition of a Non-Teacher Union and Thereafter

If the school board decides to officially recognize a union of non-teacher employees, it still retains total discretion as to whether or not to (1) negotiate, (2) meet and confer, or (3) enter into any form of a written agreement. If a written agreement is decided upon, it may range from a simple statement of recognition of the union and its ability to hold regular meetings with management to discuss issues over pay and working to a "full blown" labor contract where salary, fringe benefits, various working conditions, and a grievance procedure ending in binding arbitration are negotiated and agreed to for the stated life of the contract.

Although binding arbitration may be thought to be a valid way to settle disagreements over the terms of the labor contract, school boards need to carefully consider such because such a provision removes final decision-making authority from the board and gives it to an outside individual, the arbitrator, who most likely will apply a stricter set of arbitration principles that have been established through the case law of arbitration. (See Chapter 13 of the main text, Section V.B.)

Also, due to the Indiana Uniform Arbitration Act, IC 34-4-2, there are only five narrow reasons for which an arbitrator's ruling can be reversed. For example, an arbitrator may not be reversed for making a mistake in the interpretation of a law according to the Indiana Court of Appeals in the case of *Southwest Parke Education Ass'n v. Southwest Parke Comm. Sch. Corp.*, 427 N.E.2d 1140 (Ind.App. 1981), where the court stated at 1147 (emphasis added):

> The courts of other states which have adopted the Uniform Act and which have in their acts a provision similar to IC 34-4-2-13 agree that generally a arbitrator's mistake of law or erroneous interpretation of the law does not constitute an act in excess of the arbitrator's powers.

See the case in Chapter 13 of the main text where the school's assertion that the arbitrator was sleeping during its presentation of the evidence was not sufficient for the court to vacate the arbitrator's ruling against the school. *Ft. Wayne Comm. Schs. V. Ft. Wayne Ed. Ass'n*, 490 N.E.2d 337 (Ind.App. 1986).

III. Collective Bargaining For Certificated Employees (Teachers) under CEEBA

A. The Enforcement Agency

CEEBA contains the requirements imposed on school boards with respect to the collective bargaining process and the means by which the Act is enforced. Under CEEBA, the Indiana Education Employment Relations Board ("IEERB") serves as the state administrative agency to govern the statute's application to school employers and their certificated employees. The IEERB has essentially three general purposes:

1. Oversee the process to determine the appropriate unit and the method that certificated employees of school corporations can select (or deselect) an exclusive representative for purposes of engaging in collective bargaining;

2. Implement the method of resolving disputes during the collective bargaining process, including deciding failure to bargain in good faith

complaints and conducting the impasse processes of mediation and factfinding with its binding, last, best offer final solution process;

3. Resolve unfair practices allegedly committed by either the school employer or the exclusive representative; and

The specific powers provided to IEERB in order to accomplish these purposes are set forth in IC 20-29-3. (Its website address is: www.in.gov/ieerb.)

B. The Process for Establishing the Appropriate Unit under CEEBA

There are two methods of establishing the appropriate unit. First, the exclusive representative and the school employer may agree upon the appropriate unit. If no agreement is reached, then the IEERB will determine the appropriate unit after a hearing in which IEERB will consider:

1. The efficient administration of school operations;

2. The existence of a "community of interest" among the school employees;

3. The effects fragmented units would have on the school corporation and school employees; and

4. The recommendations of the parties involved.

The statute specifically prohibits non-certificated employees from being part of the appropriate unit comprised of certificated employees. IC 20-29-5-1(a).

C. The Process for Selecting or Deselecting an Exclusive Representative under CEEBA

1. Voluntary Recognition Based on Evidence of Representation

The school employer may recognize any exclusive representative who requests to represent a unit of certificated employees and presents sufficient evidence to the school of its representative status. Such evidence may be through a showing of interest of signed cards or a petition or other evidence that establishes a majority of the appropriate unit of certificated employees want the exclusive representative as their bargaining agent.

If the school employer believes the evidence presented to it is sufficient to recognize an exclusive representative, it must post for thirty days a public notice in each building where the school employees of the appropriate unit principally work stating the school employee organization will be recognized by the school employer as the exclusive representative of the appropriate unit. However, if the school does not believe the evidence presented to it is sufficient to recognize an exclusive representative, it must file a petition with the IEERB asserting either (a) one or more school employee organizations have presented a claim for recognition as the exclusive representative of an appropriate unit, or (b) the school has good faith doubt that the school employee organization represents a majority of the employees in the appropriate unit.

A school employer cannot recognize a school employee organization as the exclusive representative if, during the thirty day notice period described above, either (a) another organization representing at least twenty percent of the school employees in the unit files a written objection with the IEERB to that recognition request, or (b) any school employee in the unit files a complaint as to the composition of the unit with the school corporation or the IEERB.

2. Other Petitions Which Might Arise during the Representation Process

In addition to the methods discussed in Section C.1. above, the IEERB election process may be initiated at anytime through an employee petition filed with the IEERB. For such a petition to be sufficient, it must (a) be signed by at least twenty percent of the employees in the appropriate unit and (b) assert either that (i) those employees do not wish to be represented by that organization or (ii) the designated exclusive representative is no longer the representative for a majority of school employees in the appropriate unit.

Another method to initiate the IEERB election process is through a petition filed by a competing organization with the IEERB asserting (a) that at least twenty percent of the employees in the unit wish to be represented by that organization, or (b) that the designated exclusive representative is no longer the representative for a majority of school employees in the unit.

3. An Election To Determine Representative Status

Upon receipt of any such petition described in Section C.1. or C.2., above, the IEERB will investigate the petition to determine if it has reasonable cause to believe a question exists whether the existing designated exclusive representative or any school employee organization represents a majority of the school employees in the appropriate unit. If so, a hearing will be held within thirty days. Based on the record presented at that hearing, the IEERB will determine whether a secret ballot election for the selection of an exclusive representative within the appropriate unit will proceed.

A school employee organization must win a majority vote of all employees in the unit rather than a majority of those voting. For example, if the appropriate unit is comprised of one hundred teachers, but only seventy actually vote, fifty-one must vote in favor of a particular school employee organization for it to be designated as the exclusive representative of the appropriate unit. No further election is permitted within twenty-four months after a valid election occurs.

The details of the election including such things as time, place and manner of voting, permitted campaign activities, and what is in the ballot are all issues resolved by the IEERB.

D. Issues Arising in the Collective Bargaining and Discussion Process under CEEBA

1. Bargaining Collectively vs. Discussion

Quite different from private sector law governing negotiations of unions with private sector employers under the National Labor Relations Act, Indiana school corporations are not required to bargain to impasse the wide range of issues that typically comprise the "terms and conditions" of employment. The obligation of school corporations to bargain collectively is significantly different from the obligation of discussion under Indiana law.

"Bargain collectively" is defined to require the school employer (meaning the school board) and the exclusive representative, and/or their respective designated agents, to meet at reasonable times to negotiate in good faith with respect to the required subjects of bargaining (referred to as "section 4" items that consist of salary, wages, and salary and wage related fringe benefits), and to execute a written contract incorporating those matters upon which agreement has been reached. IC 20-29-2-2, IC 20-29-6-4. While neither party to bargaining is required to agree to a specific proposal of the other or make a concession to the other (IC 20-29-6-6), the impasse procedures described below are designed to compact the length of the process, "encourage" voluntary agreement, and if that does not work, require factfinding, which must conclude with the factfinder choosing the last, best total offer of one side or the other. IC 20-29-8.

"Discussion" is defined at IC 20-29-2-7 to requires the school employer, through its superintendent, and the exclusive representative to meet at reasonable times (a) to discuss; (b) to provide meaningful input; and (c) to exchange point of view on the ten subject areas of discussion identified in IC 20-29-6-7 (which following the 2011 Legislature, includes hours and teacher evaluation, but no longer requires discussion of working conditions). Discussion issues are not subject to impasse procedures. The first issue to address in the school corporation's duty to discuss obligation is, "Who is responsible to initiate discussion?" The answer is, "It depends." Generally speaking, if the exclusive representative is aware of an issue, it is incumbent upon the exclusive representative to initiate discussion. If, on the other hand, the school is considering making a change in a past practice, i.e., a course of conduct over a period of time, the school must initiate discussion.

2. Negotiations, Deficit Financing, Grievances, Arbitration, and "Fair Share"

In requiring school corporations to negotiate a collective bargaining agreement with the teachers' exclusive representative, CEE-BA narrows the school employer's required field of bargainable items to just salaries and their related fringe benefits.

The law does give express authority and responsibility to the school board to "manage and direct *on behalf of the public*" the operations of the school corporation "to the full extent authorized by law" including but is not limited to the following actions: (a) direct the work of its employees; (b) establish policy; (c) hire, promote, demote, transfer, assign, and retain employees; (d) suspend or discharge employees; (e) maintain the efficiency of school operations; (f) relieve employees from duties due to lack of work or other legitimate reason; and (g) take actions necessary to carry out the mission of the public schools. IC 20-29-4-3.

Thus, while the negotiation process results in some limitations on the school employer in its ability to act, the law specifically permits the school board to retain broad authority to run its system. One significant financial limiter under IC 20-29-6-3 is its prohibition against the board and union to "enter into any agreement that would place the employer in a position of deficit financing due to a reduction in the employer's actual general fund revenue or an increase in the employer's expenditures when the expenditures exceed the employer's current year actual general fund revenue." (The term is more succinctly defined at IC 20-29-2-6 to mean "actual expenditures exceeding the employer's current year actual general fund revenue" in any budget year.)

The 2011 amendment to the two deficit financing sections stated in the prior paragraph appears to be an attempt to modify the Court of Appeals ruling in the case of *South Bend Community Sch. Corp. v. National Educ. Assoc.-South* Bend, 444 N.E.2d 348 (Ind.App. 1983), where the court in the following passage at page 352 stated that the school district did not meet its burden of proof that it was the *teacher collective bargaining agreement* that put the district into deficit financing (bold added for emphasis):

> [T]he Board of Trustees for the South Bend school did not clearly establish where its budget cuts were implemented. The Trustees made nothing more than a bald statement that they had made all feasible budget cuts, and the only expense remaining to be cut was the teachers' salaries. The expenses of the teachers' salaries are a portion of the general fund. This general fund also covers numerous other expenses including equipment, maintenance, extracurricular activities, and other miscellaneous items. No attempt was made by the Trustees to prove which areas of the budget were cut. In this light **it cannot be said that the Trustees proved that the teachers' contract was *the expense* within the general fund which "provides for deficit financing."**

Whether the 2011 deficit financing language accomplished a legislative modification of the *South Bend* court ruling remains to be seen.

A second issue that will have to be resolved through (1) an IEERB unfair practice or factfinder decision, (2) a court ruling, or (3) a legislative change is whether a grievance procedure may legally be bargained. On one hand, the 2011 language prohibits bargaining anything *not contained* in IC 20-29-6-4 (and since "section 4" is limited to only wages and their related benefits, it does not contain anything about a grievance procedure), but on the other hand, the language in IC 20-29-6-5 expressly states that a bargained contract "may contain a grievance procedure." For 2011 at least, the law is in conflict at to whether the employer *may* bargain a grievance procedure or is forbidden to do so. IC 20-29-6, sections 4, 4.5, 4.7, and 5. IEERB's initial opinion, expressed in its FAQ document of September 27, 2011, is that a contract may contain a grievance procedure. (See FAQ # 15.)

A third issue, assuming that a contract can contain a grievance procedure, is whether it can end with binding arbitration. The 2011 amendment of IC 20-29-6-5 kept the language allowing a grievance procedure and *deleted* the words permitting it to end in "final and binding arbitration." This deletion reflects an intent that future contracts cannot have binding arbitration, but since there was no language added that expressly prohibits such, reasonable minds can disagree whether binding arbitration may or may not exist in a contract. (One thing that is clear, however, is that the teacher contract law at IC 20-28-7.5-7(c) *expressly prohibits binding arbitration of teacher dismissals*.)

Lastly, the Legislature retained the section originally passed in 1995 which makes it clear that a teacher cannot be required to join or financially support a union or pay fair share fees, representation fees, professional fees, or other fees, and that a rule, regulation, or contract that requires such financial support is void. IC 20-29-4-2.

3. Subjects of Bargaining under CEEBA

Required bargainable subjects (commonly referred to as "section 4 items") are stated at IC 20-29-6-4 as: salary, wages, and salary and wage related fringe benefits, "including accident, sickness, health, dental, vision, life, disability, retirement benefits, and paid time off as permitted to be bargained under IC 20-28-9-1."

The 2011 amendments (1) removed "hours" from the bargaining list and added it to the discussion list, (2) prohibited discussable items from being bargained, including "evaluation procedures and criteria, or any components of the teacher evaluation plan rubric, or tool," and (3) disallowed bargaining of the school calendar, teacher dismissal procedures and criteria, restructuring options available under federal and state law, ability to work with educational entities that provide postsecondary credits or dual credits, and any subject not expressly stated in section 4.

Since a grievance procedure is not stated in section 4, it would normally be prohibited from being bargained, but, unfortunately the Legislature kept section 5 of IC 20-29-6 and amended it to state that "A contract ... may contain a grievance procedure." This contradiction begs for a legislative correction.

4. General Bargaining Pointers

Bargaining itself has been described as more art than science. The school employer meeting with the exclusive representative in good faith to reach a mutual understanding over the terms of a new contract can be as simple as exchanging language and then agreeing to terms in one or two meetings or as difficult as the parties wish to make it by disagreeing over even the most mundane issues such as where and when the negotiation meetings are to occur. Personalities sometime enter into the equation. The following is a short list of helpful hints on successful bargaining.

(1) Have the right bargaining team. Credibility and professionalism mean everything. If the union negotiators distrust or resent members of the school corporation's team, it is much more difficult to reach agreement than if a level of trust exists.

(2) Be prepared - good things happen when preparation meets opportunity. School corporation representatives should have a thorough working knowledge of all aspects of the school corporation's proposal and the anticipated union's proposal.

(3) Be aware of outside influences and be ready to respond to them. School board members should have confidence in the school corporation's representatives and be willing to defer all questions about negotiations to them, notwithstanding any relationship board member(s) may have with any teachers. Moreover it is generally best that the school board not fight a war in the press and negotiate the contract in public.

(4) Be smart on language issues. Use understandable terms to describe what is agreeable to both sides. Poor grammar, confusing or complicated language, or simply not saying what you mean, can only lead to misunderstandings.

(5) Attempt to end negotiations on a high note. Position the school corporation so it can give the last thing the union negotiators want. Walking away from the table with a handshake and a desire to work together will hopefully result in a positive working relationship for the period of the contract.

5. Subjects of Discussion under CEEBA

Subjects that must be discussed by the school employer with the exclusive representative are those stated at IC 20-29-6-7 (with the 2011 added items in italics: (1) curriculum development and revision; (2) textbook selection; (3) teaching methods; (4) hiring, *evaluation*, promotion, demotion, transfer, assignment, and retention of certificated employees; (5) student discipline; (6) expulsion or supervision of students; (7) pupil/teacher ratio; (8) class size or budget appropriations; (9) *safety issues involving students and employees*; and (10) *hours*. (Deleted from the former list was "working conditions.")

6. Committee Appointments and the Duty to Discuss

Who has the right to appoint teachers to committees—the school employer or the exclusive representative of teachers? Two Indiana Supreme Court cases provide the answer, i.e., if the committee is the sole instrumentality in the **drafting and proposal** of a discussable matter, the exclusive representative has the right to appoint **all** the teachers to the committee. See *Evansville School Corp. v. Roberts*, 405 N.E.2d 895 (Ind. 1980) and *Marion Teachers Assoc. v. Marion Community Sch. Corp.*, 672 N.E.2d 1363 (Ind. 1996).

The Court's rationale as expressed in the *Marion* case at pages 1364-1365 states:

The exclusive representative may not select the school board's bargaining team or discussion team, not even one person. Neither can the school employer select the exclusive representative's bargaining or discussion team, not even one person. The right and duty to discuss are vested in the school employer (through the superintendent) and the exclusive representative.... For this reason we hold that all bargaining unit members appointed to a sole instrumentality committee for discussion between the board and exclusive representative must be appointed by the exclusive representative. How else can the exclusive representative avoid freelancing by teachers not so appointed and represent the whole bargaining unit's interests? . . .

If the Association is to conduct effective discussions with the school administration on matters discussible under § 20-7.5-1-5 [presently, IC 20-29-6-7], it must be able to appoint all those responsible for representing its members' views. The School Board cannot bring non-Association teacher voices into a sole instrumentality committee where management meets labor across the table, effectively appointing both sides of the debate on a § 20-7.5-1-5 [presently, IC 20-26-6-7] issue. This "deck stacking," as recognized by the Court of Appeals, . . ., undermines the Association's ability "to provide meaningful input" and to articulate its point of view, as required by Indiana Code § 20-7.5-1-2(o) [presently IC 20-29-2-7]. Those in the discussion committee representing the teachers' exclusive representative are entitled to management's undivided attention to its opinions and views during statutorily mandated "discussion" time. They should not have to compete in "discussion" time with views not representative of the majority of the membership.

7. Committee Appointments and School Employer's Right to Confer

The *Evansville-Vanderburgh* court in the "committee appoint-ment" case did emphasize the school employer's statutory right to confer with any person, including teachers, in the following passage at pages 901-902 (bold added for emphasis):

> Although this statute gives to the school employer the duty to bargain collectively with respect to the enumerated section 4 topics and the duty to "discuss" the enumerated section 5 topics with the exclusive representative, it also gives the right to "confer with any citizen, taxpayer, student, school employee or other person." [Presently, IC 20-29-6-9.] This is a legislative recognition of the right of all taxpayers to have some input into the operation of their local school system which is largely supported by local tax money.
>
> Both the "duty to discuss" and the "right to confer" are in the statute and both must be given effect insofar as possible. . .
>
> Therefore we hold that nothing in the statute or in this opinion would prohibit school employers from conferring with any persons they wish in order to **gather and receive information**. Basic matters of educational policy and program content must reflect the concerns and desires of the entire local community and not any one single interest group.
>
> Gathering information concerning such matters is the responsibility of the school employer. Nothing in the statute prohibits the employer from creating committees to assist it in **gathering and receiving information** which is needed to help establish or improve any matter of school concern including discussable matters. The committees may be composed of any concerned parents, students, **teachers,** experts, consultants or other concerned citizens as the school employer deems appropriate. **The committees may even be composed entirely of school employees who are not members of the exclusive representative organization as long as the committee is gathering or receiving information which is only a partial input into the final formulation of policy.** However, the exclusive representative cannot be excluded from such a committee when such committee is the sole instrumentality in the **drafting and proposal** of a discussable matter as was true in the instant case.

8. Committee Appointments and the 2011 "Proportionality Rule"

CEEBA was amended to add IC 20-29-5-7, which limits the number of teachers that the exclusive representative "may appoint to serve on a statutory or locally created" district- wide and/or school-wide committee to the same percentage of teachers at the corporation and building levels as the percentage of teachers who are members of the exclusive representative at each of said levels. The result is that the school employer may then appoint the remaining percentage of teachers.

Although the intent may have been to apply this appointment limitation for committees that are used to meet CEEBA's official discussion obligation, the statutory language does not specifically refer to a discussion committee, (nor is it even placed in the discussion portion of CEEBA). Therefore, until this ambiguity is clarified, the safer course of action if a local school created an "input" or fact-gathering committee (as opposed to a drafting and proposing one) is desired would be to create the committee by appointing teachers in accordance with the proportionality language, obtain ideas from all committee members, including teachers, form management's proposal, and then take that proposal to the official, CEEBA discussion committee, which consists only of teachers appointed exclusively by the exclusive representative.

When the committee has been created by the Legislature, such as the "P.L. 221 School Improvement Committee" (which is charged with making recommendations to the school board) could be formed and utilized in two different ways. First, it could continue to be the official discussion committee when 100% of the teachers are appointed by the exclusive representative (under the authority of the *Evansville* and *Marion* Supreme Court rulings so that there would be no duty to further discuss the recommendations). Or, in the alternative, the school employer could use the proportionality rule, appoint its allowable number of teachers, and then take the Committee's recommendations to the official discussion table where the exclusive representative has appointed all of its teacher representatives. (The second option would be a much more cumbersome and effort-burning process, and take significantly longer.)

Lastly, the proportionality rule can also be used in the exclusive representative's favor in a situation where the school employer decides to create a committee that concerns a non-discussable item. such as the school calendar. (Calendar was discussable since it was a "working condition," but this term that was deleted from section 7's discussable list in 2011.) Therefore, per IC 20-29-5-7, any school-created committee that has teachers appointed to it (even though official "discussion" is not required on the subject matter of the committee) must have the proportionate share of teachers appointed by the exclusive representative.

E. CEEBA's Bargaining Timetable and the Impasse Procedures of Mediation and Binding Factfinding

1. Sixty Days to Formally Negotiate without State Intervention

The 2011 amendment of CEEBA substantially compacted the official bargaining period when it permitted "informal negotiations" before August 1 and declared that "formal" bargaining "shall *not begin before* August 1" of the first year of the state budget biennium (which is July 1 of every odd-numbered year and August 1 of the second year of the biennium if the contract had been only for the first year or it had been for two years but provided for certain financial renegotiations for the second year). Although the statute did not set a date by which schools had to start, the IEERB has interpreted this language to require the formal process to start August 1 of the relevant year. IC 20-29-6-12. Only 60 days are given for the parties to reach agreement without state involvement. IC 20-29-6-13.

It appears that according to IEERB's interpretation, during this 60-day, pre-mediation period (as well as the mediation period), the school employer may use rainy day funds and general fund surpluses to settle the contract; however, once factfinding starts, only those funds certified by the Department of Education and the Department of

Local Government Finance (if a local referendum had passed) can be used (unless the school funding formula allows other funds to be used for specified items). (At the time of publication, this issue had not yet matured to a point of clear legal certainty.)

2. Impasse Procedures to Achieve a Contract by December 31

a. Mediation

The IEERB has the authority to mediate unsuccessful negotiations and has declared that if there is no settlement following the 60-day bargaining period from August 1 through September 30, an impasse will automatically exist on October 1 and a mediator will be assigned to work with management and the union. A mediator does not have the ability to require either party to settle on any specific term. Rather, a mediator is used to find solutions and to provide opportunities for the parties to reach common ground on as many issues as possible. Formerly, mediation was a confidential process per the terms of CEEBA, but that section was repealed in 2011, leaving it up to the common law (courts) to determine if confidentiality continues to exist.

Pursuant to IC 20-29-6-13, each party's last, best, offer must be submitted at the final mediation session (whether that session is the first, second, or third one). Only three sessions are allowed, which requires that one of two things must occur during mediation: (1) an agreement between the parties on those items permitted to be bargained under "section 4," or (2) "each party's last best offer, including fiscal rationale, related to items permitted to be bargained under section 4 of this chapter."

The above-cited code also limits the period of mediation to just 30 days, but it is unclear as to whether that is 30 days from the first date of actual mediation being held with the parties or from October 1. CEEBA at IC 20-29-6-15.1 does state that IEERB "shall initiate" factfinding 15 days after mediation "has ended" if no agreement has been reached. The more reasonable approach would be to start the 30-

day clock from the date that the parties first meet with the mediator. (IEERB's position appears to be that rainy day funds and general fund balances may be used for bargaining purposes through the period of the mediation process, but not once the factfinding period begins. At the time of publication, this is conceptually "fluid" and has not yet become a legal "stone.")

b. Binding, Final Solution Factfinding

Pursuant to IC 20-29-6, sections 15.1 and 18, and IC 20-29-8, sections 5, 7, 8, and 13.1, factfinding is a "last, best offer" impasse process designed to achieve a "final solution," i.e., a contract between the school employer and exclusive representative by the end of the calendar year. This will be achieved by either (1) the parties reaching agreement or (2) the factfinder imposing an agreement upon them. IEERB selects the factfinder, who will schedule and hold the public hearing(s), and in the absence of a voluntary agreement, will impose a new contract by selecting one or the other party's total, last, best offer, provided it does not have prohibited items in it and does not violate the deficit financing prohibition. (The factfinder cannot "split the difference" between each party's offer.)

The factfinding process begins 15 days after the end of mediation (but the first public hearing cannot start before October 1, cannot be longer than 15 days, and the last possible hearing date cannot be later than December 31).

In making recommendations, the fact-finder takes into consideration: (a) past agreements of the parties; (b) wages and hour comparisons of the employees involved with those of other employees at other public private entities doing comparable work; (c) the public interest; and (d) the financial impact on the school corporation, particularly if "any settlement will cause the school corporation to engage in deficit financing as described in IC 20-29-6-3." However, according to IEERB's interpretation, no general fund balances and no rainy day fund monies may be used to settle the contract once factfinding has started.

The factfinder issues a written recommendation to the parties and the IEERB, which may make additional findings consistent with the law and items proposed by the parties in their last, best offers. The IEERB may make the recommendations available to the public within five (5) days after issuance but must make them available to the public through the news media and other sources not later than ten (10) days after issuance. Either party may appeal the factfinder's decision to the three-member board at IEERB, but only if filed not later than 30 days after having received it.

c. Continuation of Expired Contract (Formerly, "Status Quo")

Per IC 20-29-6-16, when the current contract between the school corporation and the exclusive representative expires, this provision requires only those section 4 wages, salary and their related fringe benefit items to continue, but *"with no increase or increment in salary, wages, or benefits* for any bargaining unit employee until a new contract is executed, unless continuation would put the school employer in a position of deficit financing due to a reduction in the employer's actual general fund revenue or an increase in an employer's expenditures when the expenditures exceed the current year actual general fund revenue." (It is noted that at the time of this edition's publication, three lawsuits supported by a major teacher union have been filed against the Noblesville, Huntington, and Madison school corporations because they followed the prohibition that is emphasized in italics above.)

F. Unfair Practices Related to Bargaining and Discussion

1. The Ongoing Obligation to Bargain and Discuss

Under CEEBA, the "school employer" (i.e., the school board) has a continuing obligation to bargain any "section 4" wage and wage-related fringe benefit issues that arise during the labor contract's term. This duty arises when changes in such section 4 items are contemplated or occur and specific language in the contract does not address these changes. Should the school employer make any change to a section 4 item without engaging in the bargaining process, it may be subject to an unfair practice complaint by a "school employee" (i.e., a teacher).

It is noted that school administration, without evidence of school board approval in the minutes of the board meeting and without negotiating with the exclusive representative has made decisions with regard to section 4 wages and related benefits that have benefited teachers. Starting and continuing the practice of letting teachers on maternity leave cash in sick days to receive pay when they are no longer ill or disabled after giving birth is a common example.

Because this administrative conduct adds to teacher benefits, no unfair practice is ever filed, and the practice is continued year after year without every being added to the language of the labor contract. But, unfortunately, when a new administration or school board discovers the practice and desires to end it, IEERB decisions indicate that there is a duty to bargain and get the union's agreement to stop the practice. Although a good legal argument exists that since the school board never agreed to the start and continuation of the wage-related practice, it was never legal in the first place and, therefore, could be unilaterally stopped. No school board has ever decided to challenge any of these IEERB rulings on this basis by filing an appeal in county court.

When a change is believed needed to a non-wage item contained in one of the 10 "section 7" discussion items, the school superintendent or designee on behalf of the school employer (board) must offer to go to the table and engage in meaningful discussion of its proposed change(s) before deciding to make the change. (Or if the exclusive representative requests discussion of a section 7 matter of concern to it, the school must engage in the process.) Failing or refusing to engage in meaningful discussion may give rise to an unfair practice complaint and the IEERB requiring the school to rescind the change until proper discussion has occurred.

It is also valid for either the "school employer" (school board) or a "school employee" (i.e., a bargaining-unit teacher) to file an unfair practice against any "school employee organization," whether if be the exclusive representative or another group having teachers as its members for any of the reasons stated in IC 20-29-7-2 (below).

2. Unfair Practices by the School Employer

a. Under CEEBA at IC 20-29-7-1, it is an unfair practice for the **school employer** to:

(1) interfere with, restrain, or coerce school employees in the exercise of the rights guaranteed in IC 20-29-4;

(2) dominate, interfere, or assist in the formation or administration of any school employee organization or contribute financial or other support to the organization;

(3) encourage or discourage membership in any school employee organization through discrimination in regard to (i) hiring, (ii) tenure of employment, or (iii) any term or condition of employment;

(4) discharge or otherwise discriminate against a school employee because the employee has filed a complaint, affidavit, petition, or any information or testimony under this article;

(5) refuse to (i) bargain collectively or (ii) discuss with an exclusive representative as required by CEEBA; or

(6) fail or refuse to comply with any provision of the law.

b. A 2011 amendment added subsection (b) to IC 20-29-7-1 stating that if a complaint is filed alleging the occurrence of an unfair practice regarding an item of discussion, and the complaint is determined frivolous, "the party that filed that complaint is liable for costs and attorney's fees.

c. A seldom mentioned sentence added to the prohibition against the school employer dominating, interfering with, or assisting or giving financial support to a school employee organization states: "Subject to the rules of the governing body, a school employer may permit school employees to confer with the school employer or with any school employee organization during working hours without loss of time or pay."

3. Unfair Practices by a School Employee Organization or Its Agents

Under IC 20-29-7-2, it is an unfair practice for **any school employee organization**, or **its agents** to:

a. interfere with, restrain, or coerce (i) teachers in the exercise of their rights under CEEBA (e.g., the right to join or not join the organization), or (ii) the school employer in the selection of its representatives for purposes of bargaining, discussion, or adjusting grievances;

b. cause or attempt to cause the school employer to discriminate against a teacher in violation of the teacher's rights under section 1 of IC 20-29-7 (e.g., to join or pay fees to any school employee union);

c. refuse to bargain collectively with the school employer (e.g., engage in "bad faith" bargaining, such as insisting to impasse and factfinding that a "non-section 4 item such as hours and days must be in the contract); and

d. fail or refuse to comply with any provision of CEEBA (such as taking part or assisting in a strike, which is clearly prohibited at IC 20-29-2-1).

4. IEERB Rulings over the Duty to Discuss

a. A frequent unfair practice complaint filed with IEERB is an allegation that the school employer had failed to properly discuss a required matter. In an early unfair practice ruling, IEERB articulated its view as to what had to occur for the school employer to meet its duty to meaningfully discuss:

> Section 2(o) [now, IC 20-29-2-7], the definition of the word "discuss," indicates that the parties are <u>mutually</u> obligated "to provide meaningful input, to exchange points of view . . ." While the parties are not required to agree to a proposal or make concessions, meaningful input is more than just listening and taking unilateral action. "Input" refers to the discussion process; each side is required to put something <u>in</u> to it." (IEERB's emphasis.) *Tippecanoe*, 1974-75 IEERB Ann. Rep. 499, at 507.

Because both sides have to join in the discussion, the school employer cannot go to the discussion table with its proposed changes and essentially stonewall the exclusive representative's comments and questions.

b. Similarly, the IEERB has ruled that "meaningful input" requires something more than discussing the general or overall policy. It also means explaining the specific strategies regarding how the policy will be implemented. *Lafayette School Corporation*, 1989 IEERB Ann. Rep. 102.

c. Regarding the ability of the exclusive representative to gather information from teachers when preparing for discussion, the IEERB ruled (1) that a school employer must give the representative a reasonable amount of time to gather input from members of the bargaining unit for purposes of making discussion meaningful and (2) that eight days was insufficient to collect information on a new staff performance plan especially when days were over a holiday period. *M.S.D. Decatur Township*, 1987 IEERB Ann. Rep. 56 (1987). IEERB said:

> It has now been determined that the School Corporation should have permitted the Association to obtain input and that the Association had no duty to obtain input during Christmas vacation. Therefore, the Hearing Examiner ultimately concludes that the

refusal by the School Corporation to permit the Association to obtain input on school days from the bargaining unit constituted a refusal to discuss." *Id.*, at 64.

d. In a situation where the evidence indicated that the principal's mind had already been made up before beginning the discussion process, the IEERB found that an unfair practice was committed when the principal at the discussion meeting made statements indicating that the decision had already been reached to have large-scale teacher reassignments at the building in the fall. *Covington Community School Corporation*, 1999 IEERB Ann. Rep. 57 (1999). In an important passage, the IEERB stated:

> [S]uch action [having decided prior to discussion] would have denied the Federation its right to be afforded an opportunity to have meaningful input into the school decision-maker's though processes at a time when such input would have had the *potential* to shape or influence the ultimate decision in favor of the Federation's position.

> In other words, when a school corporation decision-maker is conceiving a change in a previous school corporation practice, he or she must present his or her proposed change to the teachers' organization for 'discussion' at a time when it is in an appropriately formative stage so that the decision-maker would still be amenable to constructive changes in his or her work product. . . ." *Id.* at 77. (IEERB's emphasis.)

5. IEERB Rulings over the Duty to Bargain

a. Bad vs. Good Faith Bargaining

The legal duty is to bargain in good faith and the IEERB in a number of decisions has stated that this determination is made based on the "total conduct or overall pattern of behavior." *Lafayette Community Schools*, 1979 IEERB Ann. Rep. 414 at 418, where the IEERB found that the exclusive representative's conduct in revoking a number of tentative agreements and then raising it prior economic offer by $40,000 was a failure to bargain in good faith. The hearing examiner stated that such actions "becomes destructive and undermines the faith and trust in the bargaining process. *Id.*

A school employer was found to have violated the good faith requirement when it "used the bargaining process over several months in an effort to attain its objective – a seven period day...The School Corporation submitted to the association increasingly one-sided bargaining proposals to pressure the Association to agree to a seven-period day. The extent of the one-sidedness ... precluded the Association from continuing to exercise its right to bargain collectively ... and proximately caused the cessation of meaningful negotiations between the parties." *Southwestern Jefferson County*, 1992 IEERB Ann. Rep. 209 at 215.

b. Refusal to Supply Information as Part of Good Faith Bargaining Duty

The school was found to have committed an unfair labor practice when it refused to release projected insurance rates to the association. IEERB stated: "As part of the duty to bargain in good faith there is a duty to provide, upon request, information which the other party needs to form positions and make informed decisions about mandatory subjects of bargaining... If the employer is in possession of information which is necessary or relevant to the union in discharging its function as bargaining representative, the employer will normally be required to turn over that information upon request of the union. ..The duty to furnish this information springs from ... [the Collective Bargaining Law] and exists independently of any duties or prescriptions under the Public Documents Act."
Charles A. Beard Memorial School Corporation, 1992 IEERB Ann. Rep. 241 at 242.

The school employer's refusal to provide access to insurance information *in a timely manner* violated P.L. 217 because the material requested was *material to the formation of the exclusive representative's bargaining position* regarding health/medical insurance. *Fort*

Wayne Community Schools, 1990 IEERB Ann. Rep. 100

c. Failing to Follow a Side Agreement as Bad Faith Bargaining

The school employer's failure to timely implement a "side set-tlement agreement" signed by the school board's and association's negotiators was found to have violated the board's duty to bargain in good faith. *Liberty-Perry Community Sch.Corp.*, 1986 IEERB Ann. Rep. 127.

In this decision, there was no argument by the school and no consideration by the IEERB of the issue of the legality of the side agreement. To comply with CEEBA, the negotiated agreement must be ratified by the school board and union, and executed by them. IC 20-29-6-6 and IC 20-29-2-2. For the board to ratify any contract, there must be evidence of approval by a majority vote of all the members of the board placed in the minutes. See IC 20-26-4-8 and IC 5-14-1.5-4(b). Absence of these indicators would mean that there is no enforce-able side agreement to the basic contract.

Also, see the case of *Evansville-Vanderburgh Sch. Corp. v. Evansville Teachers Ass'n*, 494 N.E.2d 321 (Ind.App. 1986) where the court found that a "side letter agreement" between the school and the association "was part of the collective bargaining agreement, not separate and independent in and by itself." *Id*. at 326. This quotation acknowledges that a side agreement could be independent of the mas-ter contract if it clearly states such, but this is for school drafters to make sure it so states and succeeds at getting the exclusive representa-tive's agreement.

d. "Bypass" of Exclusive Representative as Bad Faith Bargaining or Failure to Discuss

Although the term is not used in CEEBA, the concept of the school employer's "bypass" of the exclusive representative as an un-fair practice is premised on the union assertion that if the employer communicates directly with teachers regarding wage-related (section 4) or discussion-related (section 7) matters, it thereby "goes around" the union, the entity with whom the employer is legally obligated to bargain and/or discuss. Hence, if the facts indicate the employer's circumvention of the union by communicating with teachers, either individually or in groups, the union will argue that an unfair practice is committed based on a number of different sections of IC 20-29-7-1, especially subsection (5), refusing to bargain and/or discuss with the exclusive representative of the teachers.

(1) Bypass After Bargaining Has Concluded

In *Muncie Community Schools*, 1979 IEERB Ann. Rep. 371, an improper bypass was found when the school negotiated wages *directly with* six bargaining unit coaches for their participation in summer activities programs. Similarly, the same result occurred when a school negotiated with the union a *total amount* for three new extracurricular positions, but the superintendent then met with the three teachers for the positions and discussed how the amount would be divided amongst them. *Wabash City Schools*, 1976-1977 IEERB Ann. Rep. 720.

(2) Bypass during the Bargaining Process

Often times when negotiations became drawn out (which is not as likely under the 2011 compacted bargaining schedule), schools would attempt to communicate directly with teachers in hopes that they would put pressure on their union bargaining team to settle with management. Illegal bypass was found in situations where schools attached information to teachers' paychecks, called a meeting with teachers to explain management's bargaining position, gave informational memoranda directly to the teachers, the superintendent wrote teachers expressing his doubt that their union represented a majority of the bargaining unit.

After the 1979 amendment of the Open Door Law, the IEERB has not found bypass violations when the release of information was made *to the public* due to the following language of IC 5-14-1.5-6.5(a) (1):

Any party may inform the public of the status of collective bargaining or discussion as it progressed by release of factual information and expression of opinion based upon factual information.

Examples of such public release of information would be a letter to the editor, a memorandum on the schools website, and a report (oral and/or written) to the school board at an open meeting. Even though teachers may read the newspaper, visit the website, or attend the board meeting where information was released to the public, as long as the evidence indicates that the school's motive was not anti-union or to go bypass it by focusing mainly on the teachers, the Open Door Law provision protects the school from an unfair practice finding.

(3) Bypass of Discussion Obligation by Polling Teachers

While early IEERB rulings found illegal bypass on discussable topics when the school employer polled or sent questionnaires directly to teachers seeking their input, these cases have disappeared in those situations where the school's motive is merely to seek or gather information and points of view from teachers. This change resulted from the Indiana Supreme Court case of *Evansville Vanderburgh Sch. Corp. v. Roberts*, 405 N.E.2d 895 (Ind. 1980), which made clear that under the school's *right to confer* under CEEBA, it could seek input from individual teachers directly without having to go through the exclusive representative.

G. Past Practice

Past practice (i.e., an informal, unwritten course of conduct engaged in by both the school corporation and the teachers' exclusive representative) can be a dual-edged sword. On one side, the exclusive representative can rely on past practice to contest changes made by the school corporation where no discussion or bargaining occurred. On the other, the school employer may use past practice (such as utilizing the decision of a joint health insurance committee comprised of some teacher representatives) to avoid an otherwise required bargaining obligation. Due to the unique factual settings of failure to discuss/ failure to bargain claims, school corporations need to evaluate the merits of each situation independently.

A review of Indiana court rulings and the decisions of the Indiana Education Relations Board (IEERB) gives some direction on the meaning of the term "past practice." (There is no definition of the term in CEEBA.) A helpful discussion is provided in the unfair practice decision of the hearing examiner in *Goshen Community Schools*, 2001 IEERB Ann. Rep. 22 (modified on other grounds by the full board at 2002 IEERB Ann. Rep. 77). The hearing examiner stated at pages 42-44 (bold added for emphasis):

> [I]n this instance, the School Corporation made a unilateral change in a *previous course of conduct* (or in a past practice). In all prior years the School Corporation had used the reinsurance reimbursement proceeds to pay catastrophic losses: that is, losses which were in excess of the deductible of the stop-loss insurance. Based on the **prior conduct** of the School Corporation, the **teachers had a reasonable expectation** that the School Corporation would continue in 1997 to pay such losses from the reinsurance reimbursement proceeds rather than using the reinsurance proceeds to make routine monthly premium payments from which ordinary claims were paid....

In another IEERB past practice decision, *Mount Pleasant Township Community School Corp.*, 2000 IEERB Annual Report 34, affirmed at 2000 IEERB Ann.Rep. 85., where a joint insurance committee comprised of teacher and school representatives resolved changes in the health care plan, the teacher association was found to have waived its right to bargain over such changes because it acquiesced in the parties past practice of dealing with health plan issues through the insurance committee.

Indiana court rulings concerning past practice are limited. The IEERB applied the past practice concept in *Union County School Cor-*

poration, 1981 IEERB Ann. Rep. 392 (1981), reversed by the Court of Appeals on other grounds at 471 N.E.2d 1191 (Ind.App. 1984). The IEERB held that due to the school's past practice of paying teachers for working "make up" days for those previously missed due to weather-related closings in 1977-1978, the school could not unilaterally change that practice without first bargaining the issue with the union. In explaining the significance of the past practice doctrine, the hearing examiner stated (emphasis added):

> Past practices are important in that they **represent the agreed upon solution to a problem arranged between the employer and the employees.** A past practice **need not, to be binding upon the parties, be reduced to writing.** An employer or exclusive representative ignores past practices at their peril, putting at risk the relationship, or trust, of the parties. Unfortunately, in this instance, the employer simply made unilateral changes without bargaining the wages, or make-up schedule, with the exclusive representative....

The Indiana Court of Appeals first recognized and applied the legal concept of past practice under CEEBA in the appeal of the above-considered IEERB decision in *Union County School Corporation v. Indiana Education Employment Relations Board*, 471 N.E.2d 1191, 1198-1199 (Ind.App. 1984). Although the Court reversed the IEERB based on its earlier *Eastbrook School Corporation* ruling that teacher pay for makeup days is only a topic for discussion and not bargaining (since teachers had already been paid for the missed days due to the School Closing Statute), it noted that the concept of past practice was applicable to the potential "discussion" violation by the school corporation. Its analysis of the "discussion" issue was founded on the concept of past practice and the inferences which may be drawn in an instance wherein **one party disengages from the parties' past practice and thereby injures the other party, who continued the past practice based on the reasonable belief that both parties would continue it.** The Court observed that since the school corporation had paid the teachers extra for the make-up days in the prior 1976-77 year, it was reasonable for the teachers to assume that they would be paid extra for make-up days in 1977-1978. As a result of having justifiably relied on that 1976-77 past practice regarding extra pay, the teachers had no reason to seek "discussion" about that same subject in 1977-78.

The *Union County* case illustrates how flexibly the concept of past practice may be applied to prevent an injustice from occurring in the circumstance **where one party inappropriately discontinues a past practice to the detriment of the other party who in good faith believed the past practice would continue.** As a result of that flexibility, the past practice doctrine may be applied in many other factual situations to prevent similar injustices.

The main components in forming a legal standard for "past practice" under future Indiana case law are:

1. It is a *course* of conduct, where "course" is defined by the Merriam-Webster Online Dictionary as "progression through a development or period or a series of acts or events." A "course of conduct" would not ordinarily be a one-time occurrence or an action that takes place a few times over a long period of time over the tenure of a number of administrators;

2. There must be evidence that teachers had a reasonable expectation that the practice would continue, which means that there must also be evidence that they had knowledge of the practice in order to form an expectation.

3. Past practices are "agreed upon solutions" between the school employer and employees which need not be in writing. This contemplates a knowing acceptance of the course of conduct or past practice by both sides.

The Ohio Supreme Court in the non-school case of *Association of Cleveland Fire Fighters, Local 93 v. City of Cleveland*, 99 Ohio St.3d 476, 793 N.E.2d 484 (Ohio 2003), gave the following clear and concise explanation of "past practice" at page 480 (bold added for emphasis):

> Other states have contemplated the factors required for a past practice to be binding. The predominant definition. . . requires that to be binding on the parties to a collective bargaining agreement, a past practice must be (1) **unequivocal**, (2) **clearly enunciated**, and (3) **followed for a reasonable period of time as a fixed and established practice accepted by both parties.** . . .

In other words, the party that is claiming the existence of a past practice must prove that (1) no reasonable person could dispute that it exists, (2) its terms are unambiguous, and (3) both sides have accepted it as being in place for some reasonable period of time.

H. CEEBA'S Process for Resolving Unfair Practices

1. Per IC 20-29-7-4, a school employer or any school employee believed to be aggrieved by a violation of CEEBA may file an unfair practice complaint with IEERB to seek redress. The complaint must (a) be under oath, (b) set out a summary of facts involved, and (c) include the specific section or sections of CEEBA allegedly violated.

2. Upon receipt of the unfair practice complaint, the IEERB gives notice to the opposing party of the complaint and a hearing is scheduled before a hearing examiner assigned by the IEERB. Individuals may be subpoenaed to attend the hearing at which testimony is taken. The IEERB may also issue subpoenas for documents. Failure to comply with subpoenas can result in an enforcement action by the IEERB petitioning a trial court for an order against the offending party. Parties may be represented by counsel at the unfair practice hearing where the parties are entitled to cross examine witnesses. It is typical for the parties to submit post hearing briefs in support of their positions. The hearing examiner makes findings of fact and conclusions of law that are submitted to the IEERB for review and adoption.

3. The IEERB has the power to revise the hearing examiner's findings and to issue such interlocutory (temporary) orders as it deems necessary to carry out its interpretation of CEEBA's intent. The

IEERB's determination is final and may first be appealed to the trial court of either the county containing the school corporation or Marion County, where the IEERB is located. The failure of the unsuccessful party to follow the IEERB's temporary order means that the successful party must file in a county court for a judicial order to enforce the one of IEERB.

I. Internet References

The following websites may be accessed for applicable Indiana statutes in general and collective bargaining and discussion, specifically:

1. www.state.in.us/legislative/index.htm (for Indiana General Assembly main page that links to the entire Indiana [statutory] Code and Indiana Administrative [regulatory] Code);

2. www.in.gov/legislative/ic/code/ (to link to a particular title in the code, such as Title 20, the Education Code);

3. www.in.gov/legislative/ic/code/title20/ar29/ (for the Collective Bargaining Code, which is Title 20 Article 29);

4. www.in.gov/ieerb (for the Indiana Education Employment Relations Board, IEERB).

ARTICLE II

ABCs of School Law

Alphabetical Quick Reference

A

ADMINISTRATION IC 20-28-8
(See Chapter Four in the main text.)

Points of Emphasis:

A. Principal, Assistant Principal, Assistant Superintendent, and Director of Special Education Contracts IC 20-28-8, sections 1-5 and 9-12

1. The contract for these four positions is to be on the Regular Teacher's Contract form prescribed by the state superintendent of public instruction.

2. The initial contract for principals, assistant principals, and directors of special education (but not assistant superintendents) shall be the equivalent of two (2) school years, but can exceed two years if acceptable to the noted administrators and the school board.

3. The contract can be modified at any time during the term if agreed by both parties.

4. Administrators in these four positions must be notified in writing of the school board's contract nonrenewal decision *before* February 1 of the year during which the contract is to expire. If no notification is made, "the contract then in force shall be reinstated *only for the ensuing school year.*" See IC 20-28-8-3(b) for the first three positions and IC 20-28-8-11(b) for a special education director. This means that (1) the contract that was due to expire serves as the contract for the next year's period only, (2) as long as no change is made in the prior contract, the school corporation has no legal duty to follow the statutory procedure for nonrenewal in "the ensuing school year", and (3) at the end of the following year, the individual's administrative contract and duties end automatically. See *Caston Sch. Corp. v. Phillips*, 689 N.E.2d 1294 (Ind.App. 1998) where the court stated at page 1298:

> In light of the plain meaning of the word "only" and our obligation to interpret the Teachers' Tenure Law in the manner which advances the efficiency of the school system rather than the

individual teacher's rights, we believe the statute requires a school system which fails to properly notify a principal of non-renewal to continue to employ that principal for the following school year, but no longer. . . .

5. The appropriate governing body or its designee must notify the four noted administrators thirty (30) days before giving written notice of refusal to renew a contract that the governing body is considering a decision to not renew the administrative contract.

6. If the administrator is properly notified that nonrenewal of the administrative contract is being considered, the person has the right to ask for a private conference with the superintendent (or other relevant official if a special education director) within five (5) days after receiving notice.

7. The administrator then has a right to request and receive a private conference with the school board (or other managing body if a special education director) within five (5) days after the initial conference with the superintendent (or other relevant official if a special education director).

8. The rights of a principal, assistant principal, assistant superintendent, and special education director as a teacher under the teacher tenure law are not affected by the nonrenewal of the administrative portion of the Regular Teacher's Contract.

B. Superintendent Contracts IC 20-28-8, sections 6-8

1. The superintendent's basic contract must be in the form of the Regular Teacher Contract.

2. The contract must be for a term of at least thirty-six months. (This does not mean that the school board has to keep the contract at the 36 month-level each year. It does mean that if the board votes to change the duration of the contract, the minimum length has to be at least 36 months.)

3. The contract can be modified at any time by mutual consent of the superintendent and school board.

4. The rights of a superintendent as a teacher under the teacher contract law are not affected by the nonrenewal or the termination of the administrative portion of the Regular Teacher Contract.

5. If just the superintendent-position portion of the contract is to be *terminated during its term* (as opposed to nonrenewal at the completion of the contract), the school board must give proper notice and the superintendent can request a hearing ten (10) days before the termination. A hearing must be granted in an official meeting if requested and the cause for termination must be "for cause under a statute that sets forth causes for dismissal of teachers." (The causes would be those listed at IC 20-28-7.5-1(e). It is likely that a school board facing a serious enough situation to cancel the superintendent portion of the Regular Teacher Contract would go ahead and combine the superintendent contract termination process under IC 20-28-8-7 with the teacher dismissal immediate contract cancellation process under IC 20-28-7.5.)

6. The superintendent must be notified in writing of contract *nonrenewal* on or before January 1 of the year the contract expires. Case law has established that the written notice must be formal (and cannot be a personal note from a board member). Unlike *termination* of the superintendent-position portion of the Regular Teacher Contract, the *nonrenewal* process only requires a board vote and the formal notice on or before January 1.

7. If proper notification of contract nonrenewal is not made, the contract is extended for twelve months.

C. Anti-discrimination — Residence Requirements

A school board may not adopt residence requirements for teachers or other school employees. Each school corporation that fails to observe this restriction is ineligible for state funds. IC 20-28-10-13.

D. Superintendent and Principal Authority to Select and Discharge Certain Staff

The 2011 Legislature added specific employment powers regarding selection and dismissal to the superintendent for specific positions and to the principal and superintendent for other positions, **all subject to the approval of the school board.**

IC 20-26-5-4.5 reads:

> Sec. 4.5. (a) The **superintendent is responsible for selecting and discharging** principals, central office administrators, business managers, superintendents of building and grounds, janitors, physicians, dentists, nurses, athletic coaches (whether or not they are otherwise employed by the school corporation and whether or not they are licensed under IC 20-28-5), and any other employees necessary to the operation of the school corporation, subject to the approval of the governing body.
>
> (b) Subject to IC 20-28-7.5, the **superintendent and principal are responsible for selecting and discharging** teachers, teachers aides, assistant principals, building administrative staff, librarians, and any other employees necessary to the operation of the school, subject to the approval of the governing body.

This provision is significant because the Legislature for the first time has *expressly delegated the initial selection and dismissal processes to administration*, subject to the *authority of the school board to approve or reject* administration's selection and dismissal recommendations. (Therefore, the *hiring and dismissal* process cannot be initiated on the board's own motion, nor can the board substitute the names of other persons in place of those recommended by administration.) Hence, if the board rejects administration-recommended personnel, it is the administration that must start the recommendation process all over again and the status quo remains until the board finally approves who is recommended to it.

E. A comprehensive resource involving administrator, teacher, and noncertificated staff employment is the *2011 Employee Discharge Manual* published by the Indiana School Boards Association.

ATTENDANCE IC 20-33, Chapters 1 and 2
(See Chapter Eleven in the main text.)

Points of Emphasis:

A. Equal Educational Opportunity

1. The state policy is to provide equal, nonsegregated, and nondiscriminatory educational opportunities and facilities for all persons regardless of race, creed, national origin, color or sex. IC 20-33-1-1.

2. Public schools are "open to all **children** until the **children** complete their courses of study, subject to the authority vested in school officials by law." IC 20-33-1-2

a. The twice-used term "children" appears to indicate the legislative intent to limit the **right** to a public education to those under age 18 (in that the term "adult" is defined at IC 1-1-4-5(1) to mean "a person at least eighteen (18) years of age.").

b. The phrase "subject to the authority vested in school officials by law" would mean that a child who is one-week old would not have the right to attend public school because state law only permits regular education children to begin attending at kindergarten level if they are age 5 by August 1. IC 20-33-2-7.

c. As to the issue of whether or not a regular education student's **right** to attend ends upon turning age 18, or whether an adult of any age greater than 18, who has left school without graduating has the right to return for a secondary education diploma, neither the Legislature "by law" has clearly said, nor has a state trial or appellate court given an answer.

a. The State Board of Education ruled in an administrative appeal by the School City of Whiting School that there is a right to attend school at public expense regardless of the "adult" person's age. Whiting Schools did not seek judicial review to contest the State Board's decision because the Order contained a provision stating that the education that had to be offered the adult need not be in the regular school program and could be in adult evening school at public school expense. *In the Matter of Alverez and the School City of Whiting*, Indiana State Board of Education (April 13, 2000).

b. As a result of the State Board's Whiting Schools ruling, a school must enroll a person of age 18 or greater (even in instances of serious crimes, serving time, and having very few credits toward graduation) or run the risk of the person filing a complaint with the State Board, going through the hearing and State Board appeal process where the school will lose, and then appealing to the trial court in the county of the school's location in an attempt to reverse the State Board's position that all persons are entitled to attend a public school until they receive a diploma.

3. It is the policy of the state of Indiana to provide bilingual-bicultural programs for all students to aid students to reach an acceptable academic level of achievement, and preserve an awareness of cultural and linguistic heritage. IC 20-30-9-5

B. Basic Provisions of Compulsory Attendance Law

1. Application to students of school age, IC 20-33-2-6:

"A **student is bound** by the requirements of this chapter from the earlier of the date on which the student officially enrolls in a school or, except as provided in section 8 of this chapter, the beginning of the fall school term for the school year in which the student becomes seven (7) years of age until the date on which the student:
(1) graduates;
(2) becomes eighteen (18) years of age; or

(3) becomes sixteen (16) years of age but is less than eighteen (18) years of age and the requirements under section 9 of this chapter concerning an exit interview are met enabling the student to withdraw from school before graduation; whichever occurs first."

|Note: "Attend" was defined for the first time by the 2011 Legislature at IC 20-33-2-3.2 to mean:

to be physically present:

1) in a school; or

(2) at another location where the school's educational program in which a person is enrolled is being conducted; during regular school hours on a day in which the educational program in which the person is enrolled is being offered.|

2. Illegal conduct by parents per IC 20-33-2-28:

(b) It is unlawful for a parent to:

(1) fail;

(2) neglect; or

(3) refuse;

to send the parent's child to **a public school** for the full term as required under this chapter **unless the child is being provided with instruction equivalent to that given in public schools**.

|Note: There is no statutory definitions or guidelines that assist in the interpretation of the meaning of "equivalent instruction." The determination of whether or not a parent complies with this requirement when a child is withdrawn from school or not enrolled is ultimately determined via the criminal law process upon investigation by child protection and law enforcement officials under the educational neglect provision of the CHINS statute, as well as the county prosecutor if a charge is filed accusing a parent of violating the Compulsory Attendance Law.|

3. The school board is required to adopt:

a. a procedure affording a parent of a child who does not meet the minimum age requirement for kindergarten enrollment the right to appeal to the superintendent of the school corporation. IC 20-33-2-7;

b. "a policy outlining the conditions for excused and unexcused absences. The policy must include the grounds for excused absences required by sections 15 through 17.5 of this chapter or another law. Any absence that results in a person not attending at least one hundred eighty (180) days in a school year must be in accordance with the governing body's policy to qualify as an excused absence." IC 20-33-2-14(b); and

c. as a part of the written copy of its discipline rules a definition of a student who is habitually truant:

(1) Under the established definition, a student, who is either 13 or 14 years of age, may not be issued an operator's license or a learner's permit to drive a motor vehicle or motorcycle until the person is at least 18 years of age, unless by improved attendance the person has regained eligibility.

(2) Upon review, which must be done periodically, the school board may determine that the person's attendance record has improved to the degree that the person may become eligible to be issued an operator's license or a learner's permit.

(3) Before February 1 and before October 1 each year, the school board must submit to the bureau of motor vehicles the pertinent information concerning a person's eligibility to be issued the license or permit. IC 20-33-2-11

4. Exit interview requirements to withdraw from school:

Pursuant to IC 20-33-2, sections 9 and 28.5, a student who is 16 or 17 years of age is bound by the Compulsory Attendance Law, and **may not withdraw from school before graduation unless all four of the following conditions are met regarding an exit interview**:

a. the student, the student's parent or guardian, and the principal agree to the withdrawal;

b. at the exit interview, the student provides written acknowledgement of the withdrawal and the student's parent or guardian and the principal each provide written consent for the student to withdraw from school;

c. the withdrawal is due to (a) a financial hardship and the individual must be employed to support the individual's family or a dependent; (b) illness; or (c) an order by a court that has jurisdiction over the student; and

d. the written acknowledgment of withdrawal includes a statement that the student and the student's parent understand that withdrawing from school is likely to (a) reduce the student's future earnings and (b) increase the student's likelihood of being unemployed in the future.

5. Exit interview meeting (personnel and attendance requirements):

The school board must designate the appropriate employees of the school corporation to conduct the exit interviews for students. Each exit interview must be personally attended by the student's parent or guardian, the student, each designated appropriate school employee, and the student's principal.

6. Initial student enrollment requirements:

Each public school shall (and each private school may) require a student who initially enrolls in the school to provide the name and address of the school the student last attended and a certified copy of the student's birth certificate or other reliable proof of the student's date of birth. If the documentation is not provided within thirty days or appears to be fraudulent, the **school must notify the Indiana clearinghouse for information on missing children**. IC 20-33-2-10.

7. All schools' duty to send student records to a requesting school:

"A school in Indiana receiving a request for records shall send the records promptly to the requesting school." IC 20-33-2-10(d)

8. Student excusals without being counted as absent: (IC 20-33-2, sections 14-17.5 and 46)

a. serving as a page or an honoree of the Indiana general assembly;

b. serving on precinct election board or as a helper for a political candidate or party on election day;

c. appearing in a judicial proceeding upon receipt of a subpoena;

d. serving on active duty in the Indiana National Guard upon receipt of an order (for not more than ten (10) days in a school year);

e. serving with the Indiana wing of the civil air patrol (for no more than five days in a school year);

f. serving on a state standards task force;

g. attending an educationally-related nonclassroom activity under certain conditions; or

h. being excused by a superintendent, with the approval of the state board of education found mentally or physically unfit for school attendance. (An excuse under this section is valid only for the school year during which it is issued and a superintendent's action must be in accordance with limitations and regulations established by the state board concerning the procedures and requirements for the complete examination of students.)

9. Mandatory accurate daily attendance record for all schools, IC 20-33-2-20:

An accurate daily record of the attendance of each child who is subject to compulsory school attendance must be kept by every public and private school, which would include a home school. The attendance record must be made available upon the request of the public school superintendent of the school corporation where the private school is located.

10. Enforcement duties, IC 20-33-2-26:

It is the duty of each superintendent, attendance officer, state attendance official, security police officer, and school corporation police to enforce the Compulsory Attendance Law in their respective jurisdictions and to execute the necessary affidavits. The duty is several, and the failure of one or more to act does not excuse another official from the obligation to enforce this chapter.

a. An affidavit against a parent for a violation of the duty to (a) send his/her child to school under the compulsory attendance law or (b) assure that the child is receiving *instruction equivalent to that given in public schools*, must be prepared and filed in the same manner and under the procedure prescribed for filing affidavits for the prosecution of public offenses.

b. The affidavit must be filed in a court with jurisdiction in the county in which the affected child resides.

c. Any person (whether he/she is a parent or public or private school administrator) who knowingly violates the Compulsory Attendance Law commits a Class B misdemeanor, which is punishable by a fine not to exceed $1000 and/or imprisonment of not more than one year. IC 20-33-2-44.

11. Private schools not bound by state curriculum requirements, IC 20-33-2-12(a):

A school that is nonpublic, nonaccredited, and not otherwise approved by the state board of education is not bound by any requirements of the education code with regard to curriculum or the content of educational programs offered by the school. Hence, although parents must provide instruction equivalent to that of the public schools, the Legislature has clearly said that parents need not follow state of local school corporation curriculum requirements.

12. Public school discretion to enroll or permit participation of nonpublic, nonaccredited school child, IC 20-33-2-12(b):

A student who attends a nonpublic, nonaccredited school may enroll in a particular educational program or participate in a particular educational initiative offered by an accredited public, nonpublic, or state board approved nonpublic school **provided that the governing**

body or superintendent, in the case of the accredited public school; or the administrative authority, in the case of the accredited or state board approved nonpublic school **approves the enrollment or participation by the student**.

[**Note:** A comprehensive resource is the "2008 Indiana Compulsory School Att~ ~~nce Manual" published by the Indiana School Boards

B

BOARDS OF EDUCATION IC 20-26
(See Chapter One in the main text.)

Points of Emphasis:

A. Under the Home Rule Statute (IC 20-26-3), a school corporation has all powers granted it by statute or through rules adopted by the state board of education and **all other powers necessary or desirable in the conduct of its affairs**, even though not granted by statute or rule; if there is no constitutional or statutory provision requiring a specific manner for exercising a power, a school corporation wanting to exercise the power must adopt a written policy. (See HOME RULE POWERS in this Article, below.)

B. Numerous express, specific powers are granted governing bodies of school corporations pursuant to IC 20-26-5-4.

C. The state and other agencies may review or regulate the exercise of powers by a school corporation only to the extent prescribed by statute. IC 20-26-5-6.

D. The school corporation must provide a latch key program either in the school or contract with a not-for-profit organization. IC 20-26-5-3.

E. The school corporation may adopt a policy to provide athletic tickets at reduced or no charge to groups or individuals designated by the school board. IC 20-26-5-5.

F. The school corporation may appropriate necessary funds to provide memberships to state and national associations and may also appropriate necessary funds to defray expenses of attending meetings for these organizations. IC 20-26-5-8.

G. The school corporation must adopt a policy on criminal records checks, administer them uniformly and the individual is responsible for all costs in obtaining these checks. IC 20-26-5-10.

H. School board members can be paid up to $2000 per year plus a per diem not to exceed the rate approved for members of the board of school commissioners of Indianapolis Public Schools (which may not set a per diem greater than that established by the Indianapolis-Marion County Council). IC 20-26-4-7.

I. School board members cannot be disqualified on the basis of age if at least 21 years of age. IC 20-26-4-9.

J. School board members do not have to own land, but must reside in the school corporation. IC 20-26-4-10.

K. School board members cannot be an individual who is employed by the school corporation. IC 20-26-4-11.

L. When approving any contract, including those for employment and goods and services, it takes a "majority of **all** members" of the school board. IC 20-26-4-8. Otherwise, provided that a quorum (defined as a "majority of the members") is present at the meeting, only a "majority of the **members present** may adopt a resolution or take any action." IC 20-26-4-3(f).

C

CENSORSHIP (See Chapter Eight in the main text.)

Points of Emphasis:

A. Per state statute, a school corporation may allow a principal or teacher to read or post in a school building any excerpt of the 15 American history or heritage documents listed in IC 20-30-5-3(a).

1. A school corporation **may not permit** the content-based censorship of American history or heritage *based on religious references* in the 15 American history or heritage documents listed in the above-cited Indiana Code.

2. If a student uses excerpts from any of the 15 American history or heritage documents listed by Indiana Code, above, the student may not be punished in any way, including a reduction in grade.

3. A library, media center or an equivalent facility that a school corporation maintains for student use must contain in the facility's permanent collection at least one (1) copy of each of the 15 American history or heritage documents defined by Indiana Code.

B. Via a U.S. Supreme Court ruling, a school board and its administrators and teachers may censor educational materials provided a legitimate or reasonable educational concern exists (and there is no prohibition against the particular censorship in state law). *Hazelwood Sch. Dist. v. Kuhlmeier*, 484 U.S. 260 (1988).

C. Broad latitude exists for school officials to protect school children from harmful influences, especially as it relates to obscenity and sexual matters.

D. Instructional programming policies should exist for the selection and removal of curricula, books, and materials.

CHILD ABUSE/NEGLECT REPORTING IC 31-33-5 and IC 31-34-1

Points of Emphasis:

A. All staff should receive regular training concerning child abuse/ neglect reporting requirements and the recognition of the signs of child abuse/neglect.

B. All school corporation personnel who have **reason to believe** that a child is a victim of child abuse/neglect **must** immediately notify the building principal or designee. (Making the report to the principal/designee does not, however, relieve the staff member from the duty to report to child protection or law enforcement on his/her own behalf unless the staff member has reason to believe that the report has already been made.)

instant!

C. The building principal/designee **must immediately** make an oral report to the local child protection service or law enforcement agency.

D. Persons required to report are immune from civil or criminal liability; there is a statutory presumption that the report was made in good faith, and the immunity is lost only if the one who reported is found to have acted maliciously or in bad faith.

E. A person who is required to make a report and fails to do so commits a Class B misdemeanor.

F. Five of the seven required situations that are required to be reported to child services or law enforcement which are faced by school personnel who have reason to believe that:

1. the child's physical or mental condition is seriously impaired or seriously endangered as a result of the inability, refusal, or neglect of the child's parent, guardian, or custodian to supply the child with necessary food, clothing, shelter, medical care, education, or supervision (IC 31-34-1-1);

2. the child's physical or mental health is seriously endangered due to injury by the act or omission of the child's parent, guardian, or custodian (IC 31-34-1-2) [Due to the statutory definition of "custodian," a school employee whose acts cause serious injury must be reported and may be criminally charged.];

3. the child is the victim of a sex offense under the following criminal statutes:

(a) IC 35-42-4-1; (rape)
(b) IC 35-42-4-2; (criminal deviate conduct)

(c) IC 35-42-4-3; (child molesting)

(d) IC 35-42-4-4; (child exploitation and possession of child pornography)

(e) IC 35-42-4-7; (child seduction)

(f) IC 35-42-4-9; (sexual misconduct with a minor)

(g) IC 35-45-4-1; (public indecency and indecent exposure)

(h) IC 35-45-4-2; (prostitution)

(i) IC 35-46-1-3; (incest)

(IC 31-34-1-3)

4. the child's parent, guardian, or custodian allows the child to participate in an obscene performance as defined by statute (IC 31-34-1-4); and/or

5. the child's parent, guardian, or custodian allows the child to commit public indecency, public nudity, or prostitution (IC 31-34-1-5).

COLLECTIVE BARGAINING LAW IC 20-29 (See Article I in this supplement and Chapter Thirteen in the main text.)

Points of Emphasis:

A. The statutory guarantees of the **rights of employees** are to:

1. Form, join, or assist employee organizations;

2. Participate in collective bargaining with school employers through representatives of their own choosing; and

3. Engage in other activities, individually or in concert, for the purpose of establishing, maintaining, or improving salaries, wages, hours, salary and wage related fringe benefits and other defined matters set forth in IC 20-29-6, sections 4 and 5.

B. The **rights of school employers** are to:

1. Direct the work of employees;

2. Establish policy;

3. Hire promote, demote, transfer, assign, and retain employees;

4. Suspend or discharge its employees in accordance with state law;

5. Maintain the efficiency of school operations;

6. Relieve its employees from duties because of lack of work or other legitimate reasons; and

7. Take actions necessary to carry out the mission of the public schools as provided by law.

C. Collective bargaining means the obligation of the school employer and the exclusive representative of the teachers to negotiate in good faith and to execute a written contract.

D. Subjects which the school employer is required to bargain:

1. salary;

2. wages; and

3. salary and wage related fringe benefits.

E. Subjects which the school employer is **required to discuss**, and is **prohibited from bargaining**:

1. curriculum development and revision;

2. textbook selection;

3. teaching methods;

4. hiring, evaluation, promotion, demotion, transfer, assignment, and retention of teachers (which the Indiana Court of Appeals in the *Carroll Consolidated Schools* case held to require discussion of these matters only as to they pertain to "general conditions or overall guidelines," and *not* to individual teachers);

5. student discipline;

6. expulsion or supervision of students;

7. pupil-teacher ratio;

8. class size or budget appropriations;

9. safety issues for students and employees in the workplace, except those items required to be kept confidential by state or federal law; and

10. hours

F. "Work requirements."

The Indiana Education Employment Relations Board upheld a school employer when it unilaterally, without "discussion" with the exclusive representative, established a "work requirement." See *South Bend Comm. Schools*, 1997 IEERB Ann. Rep. 430, where teachers were required to collect student fees without first going to the discussion table with their exclusive representative. A work requirement is that which is "fundamental to the operation of a school system in Indiana...." *Id*. at 431. The IEERB stated at page 432 (bold added by IEERB):

> Work requirements relate to **job content** and are not subjects of discussion, unless specifically set out in Section 5 [now codified at IC 20-29-6-7] of the Act (e.g., textbook selection....

G. Strikes by individual teachers and school employee organizations, including their state and national affiliates, are prohibited.

H. "Strike" is defined to include "abstinence in whole or in part from the full, faithful, and proper performance of the duties of employment without the lawful approval of the school employer or in any concerted manner interfering with the operation of the school employer for any purpose." IC 20-29-2-16. The following actions would be a strike under the statutory definition:

1. A teacher "slow down" or "work to the contract" that limits the teachers' ability to grade and return assignments and prepare lessons.

2. The concerted use of sick or personal days that harms the efficient delivery of educational services. See *M.S.D. of Perry Township Sch. Corp. and Perry Education Assoc.*, 1980 IEERB Ann. Rep. 788, affirmed at 1980 IEERB Ann. Rep. 792, where the IEERB ruled that the exclusive representative committed an illegal strike when 52.8 % of its membership called in sick and used personal leave days on a given day.

COMPULSORY ATTENDANCE IC 20-33-2
(See ATTENDANCE in this Article, above.)

CONTRACTS IC 20-26-4-8, IC 20-28-6, IC 20-28-8, IC 20-27-5
(See Chapters Three and Four in the main text.)

Points of Emphasis:

A. School boards must approve each contract by a vote of the majority of **all of the members** of the board. IC 20-26-4-8. Thus, for a five member board, three votes are necessary, even when a mere quorum of three are present.

B. Basic contract requirements for those defined as a "teacher" are stated at IC 20-28-6. (The 2011 amendment of the term "teacher" at IC 20-18-2-22 added the clause "whose primary responsibility is the instruction of students," and expressly included superintendents, principals, and librarians. Assistant superintendents and assistant principals have statutory nonrenewal of contract protection, but if their primary responsibility is not student instruction, there is no **right** to a "regular teacher contract." However, schools are **not prohibited** from using the regular contract for positions that require a teacher license, but that do not come within the "teacher" definition for purposes of the Teacher Contract Law at IC 20-28.) Directors of special education and of curriculum and instruction are likely "teachers" because of the primary student instruction factor connected with such positions.

1. To be valid and enforceable, a contract between a school corporation and a "teacher" must be (1) **in writing** *and* (2) **signed by both parties**. IC 20-28-6-2(a) and (e).

2. The state superintendent of public instruction is delegated the authority to prescribe (1) the "uniform teacher's contract" in the alternate forms of the (a) "regular teacher's contract" and (b) "temporary teacher's contract," and (2) the "supplemental service teacher's contract."

a. The regular teacher's contract is to be used statewide **without amendment**. (No similar requirement is made of the temporary and supplemental contracts, but it could be successfully argued that the power to prescribe nullifies the power of local school officials to amend.) It is submitted that a statement placed on the contract by the school for the sole purpose of explanation does not improperly amend it, e.g., "This administrator may be called upon when the situation arises to work more daily hours than the number stated in this contract."

b. All teachers, except substitutes, employed in a public school are required to be employed on one of these three contracts. IC 20-28-6-4.

c. The temporary teacher's contract **can only be used** to employ (1) a teacher to "serve in the absence of a teacher who had been granted a leave of absence;" and (2) "a new teacher for a position: (A) that is funded by a grant outside the school funding formula for which funding is available only for a specified period or purpose; or (B) vacated by a teacher who is under a regular contract and who temporarily accepts a teacher position that is funded by a grant outside the school funding formula for which funding is available only for a specified period or purpose." IC 20-28-6-6, as amended in 2011.

(1) The specific leaves for which the temporary teacher's contract may be given are then listed, but rather interestingly, a maternity leave, i.e., the non-disability portion of the leave following the birth of the child, while not on the list of allowable uses is nonetheless universally used.

(2) The temporary teacher's contract must include "the provisions of the regular teacher's contract **except those providing for continued tenure of position.**"

(a) Due to the 2011 repeal of the former "tenure" status terms of "permanent" and "seimpermanent," the emphasized language means that there is no need to use the "decline to continue" process at the end of the term of the temporary contract.

(b) It appears, however, that a temporary contract teacher would be subject to the evaluation process under IC 20-28-11.5 (annual evaluation and rated as either highly effective, effective, improvement needed, or ineffective).

(c) It also appears that if a temporary contract teacher receives a highly effective or effective rating three times in a five year period, the person would become a professional teacher.

(d) The Indiana Court of Appeals in the case of *Ostrander v. Board of Directors of Porter County Education Interlocal*, 650 N.E.2d 1192 (Ind.App. 1995) essentially came to the conclusion that a teacher who teaches two successive years on a temporary teacher's contract, and then signs a regular teacher's contract, becomes a semipermanent teacher. However, in this case since the teacher in question had not had a temporary contract for one semester in the chain of "successive" years, she was not awarded semipermanent status. This case will no longer apply due to the 2011 repeal of IC 20-28-7 and replacement with IC 20-28-7.5.

(e) The Indiana Court of Appeals in the case of *Paul v. M.S.D. of Lawrence Township*, 455 N.E.2d 411 (1983), ruled that the Temporary Teacher's Contract Statute did **not** prohibit the school corporation from hiring a long-term substitute teacher, rather than a temporary contract teacher, to replace a teacher who had been granted a leave of absence. In essence, the court determined that if the school decides to use a written contract in such a situation, it must use the temporary contract; but if no contract is used, a substitute teacher may be employed.

C. School bus driver employees (as opposed to transportation contract drivers) must be employed on a written contract. IC 20-27-5-4.

D. Non-certificated employees are generally employed without a written contract, and as long as their employment is **not for a stated specific period of time**, they are considered "at-will" and may be terminated at any time for any relevant reason (other than an unlawfully discriminatory one, such as race, disability, or gender, or for a violation of a constitutionally protected right such as speech or religion).

However, to employ a lay coach for the "baseball season," even without a written contract, would take away the "at-will" status during that season, but once the oral contract is completed, there is no legal duty to approve re-employment; nor is there a legal duty to terminate employment because the agreed upon employment period is over and, in essence, the employment relationship has automatically ended.

E. A comprehensive resource regarding teacher and noncertificated staff employment matters is the *2011 Employee Dismissal Manual* published by the Indiana School Boards Association.

CORPORAL PUNISHMENT (See Chapter Six in the main text and DISCIPLINE in this Article.)

Points of Emphasis:

A. Corporal punishment of students has been upheld by the Indiana Supreme Court in the case of *Indiana State Personnel Board v. Jackson*, 192 N.E. 2d 740 (Ind. 1963), but each school corporation, at a minimum, should establish procedures to follow in applying it to students. Some schools have prohibited its use altogether.

B. A Beech Grove teacher's protection from criminal prosecution for battery (corporal punishment) for allegedly slapping a student's face has been upheld by the Indiana Court of Appeals in the case of *State v. Fettig*, 884 N.E.2d 341 (Ind.App. 2008), rehearing denied. The trial court dismissed the criminal charge and did not allow the issue to go to a jury.

The court's rationale in dismissing the case in favor of the teacher is expressed at pages 345-346 as follows (bold added for emphasis):

> The trial court summarized its findings in its Order granting Fettig's motion to dismiss by stating:
>
>> Here we have a classroom disturbance wherein the teacher uses some measure of touching to restore order and redirect the focus of the class. No weapons; no closed fist[;] no repeated blows; no verbal abuse; just an open handed touching to the face of a [fifteen-year-old] student which caused her face to sting...
>
> Fettig's actions fell within the bounds of her protection from prosecution for battery. **Our legislature has provided authority to school personnel to discipline students** by stating:
>
>> in all matters relating to the discipline and conduct of students, **school corporation personnel: (1) stand in the relation of parents to the students** of the school corporation; and **(2) have the right to take any disciplinary action necessary to promote student conduct that conforms with an orderly and effective educational system.**
>
> I.C. § 20-33-8-8(b). Further, Indiana Code section 20-33-8-9 provides that teachers "may take any action that is reasonably necessary to carry out or to prevent an interference with an educational function that the individual supervises."
>
> In general, **"[a] person is justified in engaging in conduct otherwise prohibited if he has legal authority to do so." I.C. § 35-41-3-1.** This statute has been interpreted to provide legal authority for a parent to engage in reasonable discipline of her child, even if such conduct would otherwise constitute battery. *Dyson v. State*, 692 N.E.2d 1374, 1376 (Ind.Ct.App.1998). Although there is a dearth of recent case law addressing the subject, **this same**

justification has long been extended to teachers as well, as long as the teacher acts within the limits of her "jurisdiction and responsibility as a teacher." *Vanvactor v. State,* 113 Ind. 276, 15 N.E. 341, 342 (Ind.1888). Moreover, **teachers are given**, in addition to the presumption of innocence shared by all criminal defendants, **a presumption of having done their duty when punishing a student.** *Id.* ...

Having reviewed the longstanding precedents of *Vanvactor*, *Danenhoffer*, and *Marlsbary*, we note that **they demonstrate the ability of the judiciary to determine whether a teacher has acted within the bounds of her authority to discipline when striking a student.** Considering the facts here-no weapons, no closed fist, no repeated blows, no verbal abuse, and the only alleged injury being a stinging sensation-in context with the right of teachers to be free from criminal prosecution for physical punishment that is neither cruel nor excessive, we conclude that the trial court did not abuse its discretion by dismissing the information charging Fettig with battery.

D

DISCIPLINE OF STUDENTS IC 20-33-8 (See Chapter Six in the main text. Also see CORPORAL PUNISHMENT section, immediately above.)

Points of Emphasis:

A. The school board must establish written discipline rules, which may include dress codes, that govern the conduct of the students, and the school board must give general publicity to the written discipline rules by either making them available or delivering a written copy of the rules to the students and parents.

B. When drafting or reviewing student discipline rules, board members and administrators should be aware of U.S. Constitution's concepts that are applicable to student discipline rules.

1. Procedural and substantive due process.

2. Free speech.

3. Vagueness and overbreadth.

C. Items that are required to be included in the student handbook are:

1. Grounds for suspension, expulsion, and other disciplinary actions;

2. Prohibition of bullying as defined at IC 20-33-8-0.2, including provisions concerning education, parental involvement, reporting, investigation, and intervention;

3. Ability to possess and self-administer medication for chronic illness;

4. Procedures for suspension and expulsion; and

5. Habitual truancy and denial of driver's license or learner's permit for 13 and 14 year old students who do not improve attendance per IC 20-33-2-11;

D. Item that should be included in the student handbook is:

Revocation of driver's license or learner's permit for students (per IC 9-24-2-1) who (1) are expelled from school, (2) receive at least a second suspension in a school year, or (3) are considered a drop out under IC 20-33-2-28.5 when they do not comply with the exit interview requirements

E. Statutory grounds for suspension and expulsion need to include:

1. Possession of a firearm, a destructive device, or a deadly weapon on "school property", which is defined at IC 20-33-8-5 as follows:

As used in this chapter, "school property" means the following:

(1) A building or other structure owned or rented by a school corporation.
(2) The grounds adjacent to and owned or rented in common with a building or other structure owned or rented by a school corporation.

2. Unlawful activity on or off school grounds, committed during weekends, holidays, school breaks, and summer when a student may not be attending school functions, if the unlawful activity may reasonably be considered to be an interference with school purposes or an education function or the student's removal is necessary to restore order or protect persons on school property;

3. Lack of legal settlement in the school corporation; and

4. Engaging in misconduct and/or substantial disobedience, *as defined by a school or school corporation's written student discipline rules*, which occurs:

(a) on school property immediately before, during, or immediately after school hours or at any other time when school is being used by a school group;

(b) off school grounds at a school activity, function, or event; or

(c) traveling to or from school or a school activity, function, or event.

F. Unlike the states of Illinois and Wisconsin where expulsions, for proper circumstances, can be permanent, Indiana students may return to school following expulsion as follows:

1. Except for an expulsion involving possession of firearms, destructive devices, and deadly weapons, a student may not be expelled for a longer period than the remainder of the school year in which the expulsion took effect if the misconduct occurs during the first semester. If a student is expelled during the second semester, the expulsion remains in effect for summer school and may remain in effect for the first semester of the following school year, unless otherwise modified or terminated by order of the governing body. School officials may require that a student who is at least sixteen (16) years of age and who wishes to reenroll after an expulsion attend an alternative program. (These expulsions are capped at two semesters.) IC 20-33-8-20.

2. For being identified as bringing to or possessing a "firearm" (defined at IC 35-47-1-5) and destructive device (defined at IC 35-

47.5-2-4) on "school property," a student *must* be expelled for at least one calendar year, with the return of the student to be at the beginning of the first school semester after the end of the one year period. (This period of expulsion, in other words, would be for a maximum of three semesters.) IC 20-33-8-16(d).

a. The superintendent is given the authority to modify the period of expulsion on a case by case basis.

b. The superintendent is required to report the possession of a firearm or destructive device to law enforcement.

3. A student who is identified as bringing to or possessing a "deadly weapon" (as defined at IC 35-41-1-8) on school property *may* be expelled for not more than one calendar year. IC 20-33-8-16(f).

G. Students who are either (1) expelled (or withdraw to avoid expulsion) from an Indiana school corporation or charter school, or (2) required to separate for disciplinary reasons from a nonpublic school or a school in a state other than Indiana by the administrative authority of the school (or withdraw from a nonpublic school or a school in a state other than Indiana in order to avoid being required to separate from the school for disciplinary reasons by the administrative authority of the school), may enroll in an Indiana school corporation or charter school during the term of the expulsion/ separation if (1) the parent informs the Indiana school officials of the circumstances in the other schools, (2) the school officials consent to the enrollment, and (3) the parents agree to conditions of enrollment set by the officials.

1. If (1) the student fails to follow the conditions of enrollment or (2) the parents fail to inform the Indiana school officials of the expulsion/ separation/withdrawal, Indiana school officials have the authority to remove the student for the length of the expulsion/separation by following the same simple process as a suspension from school.

2. The Delaware Circuit Court in the case of *William_____ v. Wes-Del Community Sch..Corp.*, Cause No. 18C01-1012-PL-0040 (Delaware Circuit Court No. 1, June 29, 2011) ruled that the school

could properly expel a student even though the student withdrew and transferred to another district in order to avoid the expulsion.

H. Any rights granted to a student or a student's parent by IC 20-33-8 may be waived only by a written instrument signed by both the student and the student's parent. The waiver is valid only if it is made (1) voluntarily, and (2) with the knowledge of (a) the procedures available under IC 20-33-8 and (b) the consequences of the waiver.

I. Statutory suspension from school is a separation from school attendance for up to ten days by a principal or designee following the designated statutory process of (1) giving oral or written notice to the student of the charges, (2) if the student denies such, giving a summary of the evidence against the student, and (3) granting an opportunity for the student to explain the student's conduct. IC 20-33-8-18.

1. This process is to precede the administrator's decision to suspend unless conditions require immediate removal of the student; in such circumstance the suspension procedure is to occur as soon as reasonably possible.

2. Following this process the administrator must send a written statement to the parent giving notice of the student's misconduct and suspension.

3. No statutory process is necessary for an "in-school suspension," but the basic rudimentary process of notice of the rule violation and opportunity to explain should be afforded and, importantly, the student should be required to perform school work while removed from class.

J. Statutory expulsion from school is a separation for more than ten days and requires a neutral party to give notice of the charges, offer and hold a meeting if requested to hear the charges of the administrator and give the student and/or parent the opportunity to respond, explain, and defend. IC 20-33-8-19.

K. An expulsion from school may be appealed to the school board, which is required to hear the appeal unless it has voted not to hear all appeals. *In Re P.F.*, 849 N.E.2d 1220 (Ind.App. 2006).

L. A principal is given the express authority to require a student of at least age sixteen who wants to return at the end of an expulsion to attend an alternative school or alternative educational program, or evening classes. IC 20-33-8-24.

M. Administrators and teachers have other disciplinary powers instead of or in addition to suspension and expulsion under IC 20-33-8-25, including:

1. Reassigning the student to an alternative education setting;

2. Corporal punishment (implied from statute, and validated by Indiana Supreme Court);

3. Restriction of extracurricular activities;

4. Removal from school-provided transportation;

5. Referral to juvenile court; and

6. Requiring a student to remain in school after regular school hours to do additional school work or for counseling.

N. School officials have the power to mandate parent participation in any action the school corporation takes to correct a student's behavior, provided the school board adopts a policy. IC 20-33-8-26.

O. If a student is at least sixteen (16) years of age when returning to school following an expulsion, the school corporation may require one or more of the following:

1. an alternative school or alternative education program;

2. evening classes; or

3. classes established for students who are at least sixteen (16) years of age. IC 20-33-8-24.

P. Regarding a principal's duty to report to the Bureau of Motor Vehicles, IC 20-33-8-33 states:

Before February 1 and before October 1 of each year, except when a hearing has been requested to determine financial hardship under IC 9-24-2-1(a)(4), a principal shall submit to the bureau of motor vehicles the pertinent information concerning an individual's ineligibility under IC 9-24-2-1 to be issued a driver's license or learner's permit, or concerning the invalidation of a license or permit under IC 9-24-2-4.

Q. The Indiana Driver's License Statute, IC 9-24-2-1 states:

(a) Before February 1 and before October 1 of each year, except when a hearing has been requested to determine financial hardship under IC 9-24-2-1(a)(4), a principal shall submit to the bureau of motor vehicles the pertinent information concerning an individual's ineligibility under IC 9-24-2-1 to be issued a driver's license or learner's permit, or concerning the invalidation of a license or permit under IC 9-24-2-4.

(b) At least five (5) days before holding an exit interview under IC 20-33-2-28.5, the school corporation shall give notice by certified mail or personal delivery to the student, the student's parent, or the student's guardian that the student's failure to attend an exit interview under IC 20-33-2-28.5 or return to school if the student does not meet the requirements to withdraw from school under IC 20-33-2-28.5 will result in the revocation or denial of the student's:
  (1) driver's license or learner's permit; and
  (2) employment certificate.

R. A student who is disabled and entitled to the protection of the Individuals with Disabilities Education Improvement Act (IDEIA) may only be suspended, expelled, or otherwise disciplined pursuant to rules of the State Board of Education, 511 IAC 7-44-1 *et seq.*

S. A comprehensive resource is the "2010 Indiana Student Due Process and Discipline Manual" published by the Indiana School Boards Association.

DRUGS, ALCOHOL, AND RELATED TESTING OF
STUDENTS IC 20-30-5-11, IC 20-33-9-1 *et seq.*, IC 20-34-2-2 *et seq.*, IC 20-34-3-18, and IC 35-48-4 (See Chapters Six and Seven in the main text.)

Points of Emphasis:

A. School corporations are required for each grade from kindergarten through grade 12 to provide instruction concerning the effects alcoholic beverages, tobacco, prescription drugs, and controlled substances have on the human body and society at large.

B. The school board is required to establish a drug-free school committee for each school in the school corporation.

C. Each committee must develop a drug-free school plan that includes collecting and reporting drug related activities in the school and addresses ways to eliminate illegal drugs and drug related behavior in schools.

D. School personnel are to report immediately in writing to a member of the administrative staff if they personally observe the use of alcohol or a controlled substance in, on, or within 1,000 feet of school property. IC 20-33-9-5

E. The administrative staff member who either personally observes a violation of alcohol or controlled substance possession or receives a report of such is to immediately report the observed violation in writing to a law enforcement officer. IC 20-33-9-6

F. The person making the written report is not liable for civil damages or penalties and is presumed to have acted in good faith.

G. The school may not send home medications with a student in grades K-8.

H. The school may send home medication with a student in grades 9-12 if the student's parent provides written permission for the student to receive the medication.

I. State and federal case law has established precedent that drug/ alcohol testing is allowed under the Fourth Amendment where (1) school officials have reasonable suspicion to believe that a student possesses or has consumed such and the scope of the search is reasonable under all the circumstances, (2) a school policy calls for random testing of students who participate in athletics and other extracurricular activities, or who drive to school, and (3) where policy allows breathalyzer testing of all students who attend a school function such as a prom.

E

EMPLOYEE EVALUATION IC 20-28-11.5
(See Chapter Four in the main text.)

Points of Emphasis:

A. Each school corporation must develop and implement (beginning with the 2012-2013 school year) a staff performance evaluation plan for **annual performance evaluations for each certificated employee** as defined in the Collective Bargaining Law at IC 20-29-2-4. (This definition also applies to those administrators whose positions require the holding of a license from the Department of Education, such as a superintendent and principal. It would also apply to temporary and supplemental contract teachers.)

B. The contents of each plan, as stated by IC 20-28-11.5-4(c), must contain the following components:

(1) Performance evaluations for all certificated employees, conducted at least annually.
(2) Objective measures of student achievement and growth to significantly inform the evaluation. The objective measures must include:
(A) student assessment results from statewide assessments for certificated employees whose responsibilities include instruction in subjects measured in statewide assessments;

(B) methods for assessing student growth for certificated employees who do not teach in areas measured by statewide assessments; and
(C) student assessment results from locally developed assessments and other test measures for certificated employees whose responsibilities may or may not include instruction in subjects and areas measured by statewide assessments.
(3) Rigorous measures of effectiveness, including observations and other performance indicators.
(4) An annual designation of each certificated employee in one (1) of the following rating categories:
  (A) Highly effective.
  (B) Effective.
  (C) Improvement necessary.
  (D) Ineffective.
(5) An explanation of the evaluator's recommendations for improvement, and the time in which improvement is expected.
(6) A provision that a teacher who negatively affects student achievement and growth cannot receive a rating of highly effective or effective.

C. If the teacher or administrator receives a rating of ineffective or improvement necessary, a remediation plan must be developed giving no more than 90 days to correct the noted deficiencies.

D. Each school corporation must report the numerical results for each performance category to the IDOE by August 1 of each year with no mention of employee names. The IDOE must post the results by school corporation on its website by September 1.

EQUAL ACCESS ACT AND STUDENT ORGANIZATIONS
20 U.S.C. sections 4071-4074 (See Chapter Twelve in the main text.)

Points of Emphasis:

A. The federal Equal Access Act (EAA) applies to secondary schools (defined in Indiana as grades nine through twelve) that receive federal funds and maintain a "limited open forum," wherein "noncurriculum related" student groups are permitted to meet.

Such schools are prohibited from denying equal access to, or discriminating against, student groups based on the content of religious or other speech at the meetings.

B. The key provisions of the EAA are set out below, with bold added for emphasis.

[1.] It **shall be unlawful** for any public secondary school which receives Federal financial assistance and which has a **limited open forum** to **deny equal access or a fair opportunity to, or discriminate against, any students who wish to conduct a meeting** within that limited open forum **on the basis of the religious, political, philosophical, or other content of the speech** at such meetings.

[2.] A public secondary school has a **limited open forum** whenever such school grants an offering to or opportunity for one or more **noncurriculum related student groups** to meet on school premises during noninstructional time.

[3.] Schools shall be deemed to offer a fair opportunity to students who wish to conduct a meeting within its limited open forum **if such school uniformly provides that -**

(1) the meeting is **voluntary and student-initiated**;
(2) there is **no sponsorship of the meeting by the school, the government, or its agents or employees**;
(3) **employees or agents of the school or government are present at religious meetings only in a nonparticipatory capacity**;
(4) the meeting **does not materially and substantially interfere with the orderly conduct of educational activities within the school**; and
(5) **nonschool persons may not direct, conduct, control, or regularly attend** activities of student groups.

[4.] **Nothing in this subchapter shall be construed to authorize the United States or any State or political subdivision thereof -**

(1) to influence the form or content of any prayer or other religious activity;

(2) to require any person to participate in prayer or other religious activity;

(3) to expend public funds beyond the incidental cost of providing the space for student-initiated meetings;

(4) to compel any school agent or employee to attend a school meeting if the content of the speech at the meeting is contrary to the beliefs of the agent or employee;

(5) to sanction meetings that are otherwise unlawful;

(6) to limit the rights of groups of students which are not of a specified numerical size; or

(7) to abridge the constitutional rights of any person.

[5.] **Nothing in this subchapter shall be construed to limit the authority of the school, its agents or employees, to maintain order and discipline on school premises**, to **protect the well-being of students and faculty**, and to **assure that attendance of students at meetings is voluntary**.

[6] **As used in this subchapter** [definitions] -

(1) The term "secondary school" means a public school which provides secondary education as determined by State law.

(2) The term **"sponsorship" includes the act of promoting, leading, or participating** in a meeting. The assignment of a teacher, administrator, or other school employee to a meeting for custodial purposes does not constitute sponsorship of the meeting.

(3) The term "**meeting**" includes those activities of student groups which are permitted under a school's limited open forum and are **not directly related to the school curriculum**.

(4) The term "noninstructional time" means time set aside by the school before actual classroom instruction begins or after actual classroom instruction ends.

C. The U.S. Supreme Court upheld the constitutionality of the Equal Access Act due to its secular purpose of protecting private student speech, and ruled the school in violation when it denied access to a student group that sought to meet for religious purposes. *Mergens v. Board of Educ.*, 496 U.S. 226 (1990).

1. In addressing the issue of whether the school had created a "limited open forum," the Court stated that such a forum is created if the school sponsors clubs or permits groups to meet that are **not directly related to its curriculum offerings**.

2. Since such non-curriculum-related groups as scuba diving, chess and a service club that worked with special education classes were allowed to meet, a "limited open forum" was created and, therefore, it violated the Act to prohibit a student-initiated religious group from meeting.

EQUAL EDUCATIONAL OPPORTUNITIES IC 20-33-1
(See Chapter Nine in the main text and the section on
ATTENDANCE in this Article.)

EXPULSIONS AND SUSPENSIONS
(See Chapter Six in the main text, and the sections on DISCIPLINE and PROCEDURAL DUE PROCESS in this Article.)

F

FAMILY EDUCATIONAL RIGHTS AND PRIVACY ACT (FERPA) 20 U.S.C. 1232g; Indiana Parental Access to Student Records IC 20-33-7

Points of Emphasis:

A. Under FERPA, a federal statute, school boards must enact policies to establish a process for giving notice to parents and "eligible students" (those at least 18 years of age) of their right to inspect, review, and challenge the content of a student's "education record."

B. The general rule under FERPA is that an education record of a student is confidential unless (1) the parent or eligible student grants written consent for disclosure or (2) the record is disclosed pursuant to one of the exceptions under the law.

C. Under Indiana's much shorter version of FERPA at IC 20-33-7, the statute:

1. applies to all nonpublic schools and public schools (whereas FERPA applies only to schools that receive federal funds);

2. gives noncustodial parents the "same access" to the education record, which expands rights given under FERPA. * Stepparents, divorced parents.

a. FERPA limits both custodial and noncustodial parents to the right **only of inspection and review** of an education record, and **not the right to a** copy. The one exception that permits them to receive a copy is when circumstances are such that they are unable to or it would be very difficult for them to come to school to inspect and review the record. *Seems vague

b. Under Indiana's "same access" requirement, however, if the custodial parent is mailed a copy of a report card, for example, the noncustodial parent has the same right to have the record mailed (even if the noncustodial parent lives next door to the school).

3. Indiana's version permits certain disclosures of education record information to juvenile justice agency officials under the following conditions as stated in IC 20-33-7-3(b) and (c):

> A school corporation or other entity to which the education records privacy provisions of the federal Family Educational Rights and Privacy Act (20 U.S.C. 1232g) apply may disclose or report on the education records of a child, including personally identifiable information contained in the education records, without the consent of the child's parent under the following conditions:
>
> (1) The disclosure or reporting of education records is to a state or local juvenile justice agency.
> (2) The disclosure or reporting relates to the ability of the juvenile justice system to serve, before adjudication, the student whose records are being released.
> (3) The juvenile justice agency receiving the information certifies, in writing, to the entity providing the information that the agency or individual receiving the information has agreed not to disclose it to a third party, other than another juvenile justice agency, without the consent of the child's parent.
> (c) For purposes of subsection (b)(2), a disclosure or reporting of education records concerning a child who has been adjudicated as a delinquent child shall be treated as related to the ability of the juvenile justice system to serve the child before adjudication if the juvenile justice agency seeking the information provides sufficient information to enable the keeper of the education records to determine that the juvenile justice agency seeks the information in order to identify and intervene with the child as a juvenile at risk of delinquency rather than to obtain information solely related to supervision of the child as an adjudicated delinquent child.

D. The following selected FERPA regulations at Title 34 of the Code of Federal Regulations ("CFR"), section 99 (34 CFR sec. 99.1 *et seq.*) are very relevant to the understanding of the statute and are followed with commentary by the writer of this supplement (bold print added for emphasis with regulations appearing in italics):

1. Definitions. *Sec. 99.3 What definitions apply to these regulations?*

Directory information *means information contained in an education record of a student that would not generally be considered harmful or an invasion of privacy if disclosed. It includes, but is not limited to, the student's name, address, telephone listing, electronic mail address, photograph, date and place of birth, major field of study, dates of attendance, grade level, enrollment status (e.g., undergraduate or graduate; full-time or part-time), participation in officially recognized activities and sports, weight and height of members of athletic teams, degrees, honors and awards received, and the most recent educational agency or institution attended.*

Items contained in a school's notice of "directory information" are a major exception to FERPA's rule that written consent must be obtained before disclosing an "education record." As long as the school notifies parents and eligible students of what is contained in this exception, and allows parents to "opt out" of the exception, the school may disclose any of the listed information. The federal definition may be modified locally, and it is recommended that the following language be considered for inclusion in the above definition after "photograph":

> "and video recording not used in a disciplinary matter, student work displayed at the discretion of the teacher with no grade displayed,"

By including the terms photograph and video recording, as well as displayed student work in "directory information," it means that this information may be disclosed without the written consent of the parent or eligible student (unless under section 99.37, either person states in writing that such record is not to be disclosed). Thus, unless the parent or eligible student has given written notice of the types of directory information that are **not** to be disclosed, no consent would be needed to display student pictures or student-created work in school yearbooks, newspapers, webpages, bulletin boards, album covers, music performance DVD's, graduation ceremonies, etc. Additionally, by stating "not used in a disciplinary matter" after "photograph and video recording," it would prevent a media reporter, for example, from gaining access to a school bus

written consent for yearbook photo!

or hallway recording showing a fight between two students which resulted in discipline.

*Education records. (a) The term means those records that are: (1) Directly related to a student; and (2) **Maintained** by an educational agency or institution or by a party acting for the agency or institution. (b) The term does **not** include: (1) Records that are **kept in the sole possession of the maker, are used only as a personal memory aid, and are not accessible or revealed to any other person except a temporary substitute** for the maker of the record. . . .*

To be an "education record," the record must be "maintained," a term that neither FERPA nor its regulations define. The Supreme Court in *Owasso Independent Sch. Dist. v. Falvo,* 534 U.S. 426, 433 (2002), quoting the Random House Dictionary, said that the ordinary meaning of "maintain" is "'to keep in existence or continuance; preserve; retain.'" The Court also stated at page 433:

> The word 'maintain' suggests FERPA records will be kept in a filing cabinet in a records room at the school or on a permanent secure database, perhaps even after the student is no longer enrolled. The student graders only handle assignments for a few moments as the teacher calls out the answers. It is fanciful to say they maintain the papers in the same way the registrar maintains a student's folder in a permanent file.

In the *Falvo* case, the Supreme Court decided that the school did not violate FERPA's student record confidentiality provisions when it allowed teachers to have students grade each others papers and then report the grade in front of all the students to the teacher who recorded it in the grade book. The Court based its ruling on the lack of any evidence that the school "maintained" these daily grades or the grade books in which they were kept and, thus, they were not "education records." However, where a school does in fact keep grade books, the daily grades kept therein would be "education records," and it would violate FERPA to allow teachers to have students' grades each others papers.

As to displayed student work on classroom walls, it is reasonable to conclude from the *Falvo* case that since such displayed material is only kept by the school for a brief period of time because it is returned to the student, it is not "maintained," and hence is never an "education record." If not such a record, there would be no violation of FERPA in displaying it.

Parent means a parent of a student and includes a natural parent, a guardian, or an individual acting as a parent in the absence of a parent or a guardian.

The FERPA definition of "parent" is much broader than the Indiana statutory definition at IC 20-18-2-13. As a result, for example, a school may exclude a non-custodial parent from a parent-teacher conference (because the person would not be a "parent" under the State definition). However, the school could not prevent the noncustodial parent under FERPA from inspecting and reviewing his/her child's education records unless there was knowledge of a court order or other legally binding document relating to divorce, separation, or custody that prohibits access to the records.

Personally identifiable information includes, but is not limited to: (a) The student's name; (b) The name of the student's parent or other family member; (c) The address of the student or student's family; (d) **A personal identifier, such as the student's social security number or student number; (e) A list of personal characteristics that would make the student's identity easily traceable; or (f) Other information that would make the student's identity easily traceable.**

2. Sec. 99.5 What are the rights of students?

(a) When a student becomes an eligible student, the rights accorded to, and consent required of, parents under this part transfer from the parents to the student. (b) The Act and this part do not prevent educational agencies or institutions from giving students rights in addition to those given to parents. . . .

Although FERPA rights transfer automatically from parents to the 18-year-old student, Sec. 99.31(a)(8) of the Regulations makes clear that as long as the student is still a "dependent" of the parent for federal income tax purposes, the school **may** (but is not required to) release education records to the parent without the student's prior written consent.

3. Sec. 99.7   What must an educational agency or institution include in its annual notification?

*(a)(1)   Each educational agency or institution **shall annually notify** parents of students currently in attendance, or eligible students currently in attendance, of their rights under the Act and this part.   (2) The notice **must inform parents or eligible students that they have the right** to— (i) **Inspect and review** the student's education records; (ii) **Seek amendment** of the student's education records that the parent or eligible student believes to be inaccurate, misleading, or otherwise in violation of the student's privacy rights; (iii) **Consent to disclosures of personally identifiable information contained in the student's education records**, except to the extent that the Act and Sec. 99.31 authorize disclosure without consent; and (iv) **File with the Department a complaint** under Sec. Sec. 99.63 and 99.64 concerning alleged failures by the educational agency or institution to comply with the requirements of the Act and this part.(3) The **notice must include all of the following**: (i) The procedure for exercising the right to inspect and review education records (ii) The procedure for requesting amendment of records under Sec. 99.20. (iii) If the educational agency or institution has a policy of disclosing education records under Sec. 99.31(a)(1), **a specification of criteria for determining who constitutes a school official and what constitutes a legitimate educational interest**. (b) An educational agency or institution may provide this notice by any means that are reasonably likely to inform the parents or eligible students of their rights. (1) An educational agency or institution shall effectively notify parents or eligible students who are disabled. (2) An agency or institution of elementary or secondary education shall effectively notify parents who have a primary or home language other than English.*

School boards need to have adopted language similar to the following in order to comply with the **requirement to specify criteria for those who are school officials and what constitutes a legitimate**

educational interest for school personnel to legally gain access to education records:

> One exception which permits disclosure without consent is disclosure to school officials with legitimate educational interests. Such a school official is defined as a person employed by the School Corporation as an administrator, supervisor, instructor, or support staff member (including health or medical staff and law enforcement unit personnel); a person serving on the School Board; a person or company with whom the School Corporation has contracted to perform a special task (such as an attorney, auditor, medical consultant, therapist, or data storage/retrieval firm); or a parent or student serving on an official committee (such as a disciplinary or grievance committee), or assisting another school official in performing his or her tasks.

A school official has a legitimate educational interest if the official needs to review an education record in order to fulfill his or her professional responsibility. For example, a third grade teacher wanting to see how a particular student in last year's class is doing as a fourth grader is a "school official," but would **not** have a "legitimate educational interest" in checking any education records of that student.

4. Sec. 99.12 What limitations exist on the right to inspect and review records?

(a) If the education records of a student contain information on more than one student, the parent or eligible student may inspect and review or be informed of only the specific information about that student. . . .

If the education record is a picture or video recording, **and the school has not expressly listed these in its definition of directory information**, the requesting party (parent or eligible student) is only entitled to see the image of the parent's child or the eligible student him/herself. For a video recording, this requires schools to either us "blur out" technology or improvise by cutting a hole in a piece of cardboard and move the hole so that only the one student is able to be viewed (unless the other affected persons give written consent that others may be viewed).

5. *Sec. 99.30   Under what conditions is prior consent required to disclose information?*

(a) The parent or eligible student shall provide a signed and dated written consent before an educational agency or institution discloses personally identifiable information from the student's education records, except as provided in Sec. 99.31. (b) The written consent must: (1) Specify the records that may be disclosed; (2) State the purpose of the disclosure; and (3) Identify the party or class of parties to whom the disclosure may be made. (c) When a disclosure is made under paragraph (a) of this section: (1) If a parent or eligible student so requests, the educational agency or institution shall provide him or her with a copy of the records disclosed; and (2) If the parent of a student who is not an eligible student so requests, the agency or institution shall provide the student with a copy of the records disclosed. (d) ``Signed and dated written consent'' under this part may include a record and signature in electronic form that— (1) Identifies and authenticates a particular person as the source of the electronic consent; and (2) Indicates such person's approval of the information contained in the electronic consent.

6. *Sec. 99.31   Under what conditions is **prior consent not required** to disclose information?*

*(a) An educational agency or institution may disclose personally identifiable information from an education record of a student without the consent required by Sec. 99.30 **if the disclosure meets one or more of the following conditions:***

*(1) The disclosure is to **other school officials, including teachers,** within the agency or institution whom the **agency or institution has determined to have legitimate educational interests.***

*(2) The disclosure is, subject to the requirements of Sec. 99.34, to **officials of another school, school system, or institution of postsecondary education where the student seeks or intends to enroll.***

(3) The disclosure is, subject to the requirements of Sec. 99.35, to authorized representatives of— (i) The Comptroller General of the United States; (ii) The Attorney General of the United States; (iii) The

Secretary; or (iv) State and local educational authorities.

(4)(i) The disclosure is in connection with financial aid for which the student has applied or which the student has received, if the information is necessary for such purposes as to: (A) Determine eligibility for the aid; (B) Determine the amount of the aid; (C) Determine the conditions for the aid; or (D) Enforce the terms and conditions of the aid...

(5)(i) The disclosure is to State and local officials or authorities to whom this information is specifically— ... (B) Allowed to be reported or disclosed pursuant to State statute adopted after November 19, 1974, subject to the requirements of Sec. 99.38...

(6)(i) The disclosure is to organizations conducting studies for, or on behalf of, educational agencies or institutions to: (A) Develop, validate, or administer predictive tests; (B) Administer student aid programs; or (C) Improve instruction. (ii) The agency or institution may disclose information under paragraph (a)(6)(i) of this section only if: (A) The study is conducted in a manner that does not permit personal identification of parents and students by individuals other than representatives of the organization; and (B) The information is destroyed when no longer needed for the purposes for which the study was conducted...

(7) The disclosure is to accrediting organizations to carry out their accrediting functions.

*(8) The disclosure is to **parents, as defined in Sec. 99.3, of a dependent student, as defined in section 152 of the Internal Revenue Code of 1986.***

*(9)(i) The disclosure is to **comply with a judicial order or lawfully issued subpoena**. (ii) The educational agency or institution may disclose information under paragraph (a)(9)(i) of this section only if the agency or institution makes a reasonable effort to notify the parent or eligible student of the order or subpoena in advance of compliance, so that the parent or eligible student may seek protective action, unless the disclosure is in compliance with— (A) A Federal grand jury subpoena and the court has ordered that the existence or the contents of the subpoena or the information furnished in response*

to the subpoena not be disclosed; or (B) Any other subpoena issued for a law enforcement purpose and the court or other issuing agency has ordered that the existence or the contents of the subpoena or the information furnished in response to the subpoena not be disclosed. (iii)(A) If an educational agency or institution initiates legal action against a parent or student, the educational agency or institution may disclose to the court, without a court order or subpoena, the education records of the student that are relevant for the educational agency or institution to proceed with the legal action as plaintiff. (B) If a parent or eligible student initiates legal action against an educational agency or institution, the educational agency or institution may disclose to the court, without a court order or subpoena, the student's education records that are relevant for the educational agency or institution to defend itself.

(10) The disclosure is in connection with a **health or safety emergency**, *under the conditions described in Sec. 99.36.*

(11) The disclosure is **information the educational agency or institution has designated as ``directory information''**, *under the conditions described in Sec. 99.37.*

(12) The disclosure is to **the parent of a student who is not an eligible student or to the student**. . . . [Remainder omitted.]

Regarding subsection (1), suggested language defining "legitimate educational interests" appears in item number 3, above. Clearly a school employee who learns something from an education record of a particular student is permitted to share that information (orally or in writing) with those who have "legitimate educational interests." However, that information could not be legally shared with a "nosy" employee who wanted the information on a particular student for personal reasons. An employee who discloses information from an education record to anyone not having "legitimate educational interests violates FERPA.

Regarding subsection (5), since Indiana adopted a law in 2001 permitting "juvenile justice agency" personnel to seek information from education records of students suspected of committing acts of juvenile delinquency, it is permissible to disclose such without the written consent of the parent as long as the juvenile agency representative (e.g., law enforcement or probation) sign a form with specific stipulations. Indiana Code 20-33-7-3 is the statute that allows a school to release education records without parental consent to a state or local juvenile justice agency that requests such records from the school. Certain conditions must be met before the release of the records is made. The person requesting such records must certify in writing that the records will not be disclosed to a third party without the consent of the student's parent, guardian or custodian **and** the records must be used only for the purpose of serving the student prior to the student being adjudicated a delinquent child. A school's student records policy needs to include the following or similar language:

Where disclosure is to a state or local juvenile justice agency and relates to the ability of such agency to serve before adjudication the student whose records are being released and such agency receiving the information certifies in writing that the agency has agreed not to disclose it to a third party without the consent of the student's parent, guardian, or custodian. Such information may not be used to aid in the supervision of a delinquent child.

Subsection (8) permits the school, once a student turns age 18 and becomes an "eligible student," to continue sharing the student's education records with the parents without having to get the eligible student's written consent, as long as the student is still a "dependent" for federal income tax purposes (i.e., the parent may still claim the student as a tax deduction).

Subsection (11)'s "directory information" exception is the probably the most expansive and utilized of all. The key is giving annual notice to parents of how the term is defined by each school district. Absent this notice, the exception will not exist, and a school will violate FERPA in such a simple situation as disclosing the student's name on the honor roll. The directory information notice must give an opportunity for a parent or eligible student (one who is 18 or older) to choose to "opt out" of any of the exceptions by a date that the school states in the notice. Hence, a parent not wanting a child's photograph or video image (that is listed as directory information) disclosed, and who notifies the school of such, can prohibit the school's disclosure of such record without the parent's written consent. (This is tough to keep track of and would apply to, say, one student in a group picture that the school would like to place on its web page.

Either the student's face, and perhaps body if it would make the student identifiable, would have to be covered or removed or not use the picture at all.)

7. Sec. 99.36 What conditions apply to disclosure of information in health and safety emergencies?

*(a) An educational agency or institution may disclose personally identifiable information from an education record **to appropriate parties** in connection with an emergency **if knowledge of the information is necessary to protect the health or safety of the student or other individuals**.*

(b) Nothing in this Act or this part shall prevent an educational agency or institution from— (1) Including in the education records of a student appropriate information concerning disciplinary action taken against the student for conduct that posed a significant risk to the safety or well-being of that student, other students, or other members of the school community; (2) Disclosing appropriate information maintained under paragraph (b)(1) of this section to teachers and school officials within the agency or institution who the agency or institution has determined have legitimate educational interests in the behavior of the student; or (3) Disclosing appropriate information maintained under paragraph (b)(1) of this section to teachers and school officials in other schools who have been determined to have legitimate educational interests in the behavior of the student. (c) Paragraphs (a) and (b) of this section will be strictly construed.

Law enforcement and health officials would be "appropriate parties" for purposes of this provision. However, before releasing health-related information from a student's education record, the school official must be reasonably certain that an emergency exists. Knowing that a responsible student has HIV-AIDS by itself would not constitute an emergency that would allow the disclosure to health officials without having the parent's or eligible student's written consent.

8. *Sec. 99.37   What conditions apply to disclosing directory information?*

(a) An educational agency or institution may disclose directory information **if it has given public notice to parents of students in attendance and eligible students in attendance** *at the agency or institution of:* **(1) The types of personally identifiable information that the agency or institution has designated as directory information; (2) A parent's or eligible student's right to refuse to let the agency or institution designate any or all of those types of information about the student as directory information; and (3) The period of time within which a parent or eligible student has to notify the agency or institution in writing that he or she does not want any or all of those types of information about the student designated as directory information.** *(b) An educational agency or institution may disclose directory information about former students without meeting the conditions in paragraph (a) of this section.*

9. Sec. 99.38   What conditions apply to disclosure of information as permitted by State statute adopted after November 19, 1974, concerning the juvenile justice system?

(a) If reporting or disclosure allowed by State statute concerns the juvenile justice system and the system's ability to effectively serve, prior to adjudication, the student whose records are released, an educational agency or institution may disclose education records under Sec. 99.31(a)(5)(i)(B).

(b) The officials and authorities to whom the records are disclosed shall certify in writing to the educational agency or institution that the information will not be disclosed to any other party, except as provided under State law, without the prior written consent of the parent of the student. . . .

FIELD TRIPS (See Chapter Two in the main text and NEGLIGENCE in this Article, below.)

FREEDOM OF EXPRESSION FOR STUDENTS AND EMPLOYEES (See Chapter Three and Chapter Eight in the main text.)

Points of Emphasis:

A. The First Amendment to the federal constitution guarantees freedom of speech (as does the Indiana Constitution at Article 1, Section 9).

B. Students have no free expression right to engage in defamatory, obscene, lewd, vulgar, indecent or inflammatory expression in public schools. *Tinker v. Des Moines Independent School District*, 393 U.S. 503 (1969); *Bethel Sch. Dist. v. Fraser*, 478 U.S. 675 (1986).

1. Neither can students promote or advocate illegal drug or alcohol use. *Morse v. Frederick*, 551 U.S. 393 (2007).

2. Student speech in **school sponsored speech activities** (such as the school newspaper or a student government election process) may be regulated and disciplined provided the school has a **"legitimate pedagogical concern,"** (a much less demanding standard than *Tinker's* **substantial disruption or a reasonable forecast thereof**. *Hazelwood Sch. Dist. v. Kuhlmeier*, 484 U.S. 260 (1988).

3. Freedom of speech entitles a student to sit (quietly and respectfully) and not participate in the Pledge of Allegiance. *West Virginia State Bd. of Educ. v. Barnette*, 319 U.S. 624 (1943).

C. Landmark cases in the United States Supreme Court impacting school employee freedom of speech:

1. *Pickering v. Board of Education*, 391 U.S. 563 (1968) concerning public school teachers' right to speak as **citizens** (but not as employees within their job duties) on matters of **public** (but not personal) concern, provided that the public school's interest in its efficient operation is not threatened or impaired by the speech;

2. *Mt. Healthy City School District v. Doyle*, 429 U.S. 274 (1977), regarding school officials' ability to legally discipline and discharge an employee if sufficient cause exists independent of the protected speech;

3. *Garcetti v. Ceballos*, 547 U.S. 410 (2006), where the Court ruled that since a deputy district attorney's memo (which created the controversy) was written as **part of his employment duties,** he was speaking as a government **employee** and **not as a citizen,** and, therefore, his reassignment, transfer, and denial of promotion for having written the memo did not violate any speech rights.

FREEDOM OF RELIGION
(See Chapter Twelve in the main text.)

Points of Emphasis:

A. In order to promote **religious neutrality** by the federal and state governments, the First Amendment of the U.S. Constitution guarantees the free exercise of religion as a fundamental right, and for this reason, prohibits government from the "establishment of religion." (Also see Article 1, Sections 3 and 4 of the Indiana Constitution.)

As to the meaning and application of the prohibition against religious establishment by governmental bodies, their officials, and employees, the Supreme Court in *Everson v. Board of Education*, 330 U.S. 1, 15-16 (1947), stated (bold added for emphasis):

> The "establishment of religion" clause of the First Amendment means at least this: **neither a state nor the Federal Government can set up a church.** Neither **can pass laws that aid one religion, aid all religions, or prefer one religion over another.** Neither **can force nor influence a person to go to or to remain away from church against his will or force him to profess a belief or disbelief in any religion. No person can be punished for entertaining or professing religious beliefs or disbeliefs, for church attendance or non-attendance. No tax in any amount, large or small, can be levied to support any religious activities**

or institutions, whatever they may be called, or whatever form they may adopt to teach or practice religion. Neither a state nor the Federal Government can, openly or secretly, participate in the affairs of any religious organizations or groups, and vice versa. In the words of Jefferson, the clause against establishment of religion by law was intended to erect "a wall of separation between church and State." . . .

B. Major Supreme Court religion cases affecting public schools include:

1. *Pierce v. Society of Sisters*, 268 U.S. 510 (1925), upheld the right of parents to send their children to religious schools by invalidating an Oregon statute that mandated students to attend public schools only.

2. *Everson v. Board of Education*, 330 U.S. 1 (1947), upheld a New Jersey statute that reimbursed parents of parochial school students for public transportation costs (because the program was neutral by also reimbursing parents of public school children, did not fund religious education, and was consistent with its *Pierce* ruling that parents had the right to send their children to religious schools).

3. *McCollum v. Board of Education*, 333 U.S. 203 (1948), invalidated a Champaign, Illinois district's program of having religious teachers of various faiths come into its public schools and substitute religious education for secular education one day a week (because it utilized "the tax-established and tax-supported public school system to aid religious groups to spread their faith" which violated the establishment of religion clause).

4. *Zorach v. Clauson*, 343 U.S. 306 (1952), upheld New York City Schools "released-time" program for religious education based on rationale stated at page 684:

> The government must be neutral when it comes to competition between sects. It may not thrust any sect on any person. It may not make a religious observance compulsory. It may not coerce anyone to attend church, to observe a religious holiday, or to take religious instruction. But it can close its doors or suspend its operations as to those who want to repair to their religious sanctuary for worship

or instruction. No more than that is undertaken here.

5. *Engle v. Vitale*, 370 U.S. 421 (1962), struck down a New York school board's directive that the following prayer be recited by every class at the start of each school day:

> Almighty God, we acknowledge our dependence upon Thee, and we beg Thy blessings upon us, our parents, our teachers and our Country.

The Court's thinking was expressed at page 424:

> We think that by using its public school system to encourage recitation of the Regents' prayer, the State of New York has adopted a practice wholly inconsistent with the Establishment Clause. There can, of course, be no doubt that New York's program of daily classroom invocation of God's blessings as prescribed in the Regents' prayer is a religious activity. It is a solemn avowal of divine faith and supplication for the blessings of the Almighty.

6. *School Dist. of Abington Tp., Pa. v. Schempp*, 374 U.S. 203 (1963), overturned a Pennsylvania statute stating that "At least ten verses from the Holy Bible shall be read, without comment, at the opening of each public school on each school day." The Court stated part of its rationale at page 222:

> The wholesome 'neutrality' of which this Court's cases speak thus stems from a recognition of the teachings of history that powerful sects or groups might bring about a fusion of governmental and religious functions or a concert or dependency of one upon the other to the end that official support of the State or Federal Government would be placed behind the tenets of one or of all orthodoxies. This the Establishment Clause prohibits. And a further reason for neutrality is found in the Free Exercise Clause, which recognizes the value of religious training, teaching and observance and, more particularly, the right of every person to freely choose his own course with reference thereto, free of any compulsion from the state. This the Free Exercise Clause guarantees.

7. *Epperson v. State of Ark.*, 393 U.S. 97 (1968), struck down Arkansas statutes that made it a misdemeanor to teach evolution in public schools and in colleges and universities supported in whole or in part by public funds. The basis for the Court's ruling was grounded on the aiding of religion by the state and breaching the neutrality requirement of the religion clauses. The Court stated at pages 108-109:

> [T]here can be no doubt that Arkansas has sought to prevent its teachers from discussing the theory of evolution because it is contrary to the belief of some that the Book of Genesis must be the exclusive source of doctrine as to the origin of man. No suggestion has been made that Arkansas' law may be justified by considerations of state policy other than the religious views of some of its citizens. It is clear that fundamentalist sectarian conviction was and is the law's reason for existence. Its antecedent, Tennessee's 'monkey law,' candidly stated its purpose: to make it unlawful 'to teach any theory that denies the story of the Divine Creation of man as taught in the Bible, and to teach instead that man has descended from a lower order of animals. Perhaps the sensational publicity attendant upon the Scopes trial induced Arkansas to adopt less explicit language. It eliminated Tennessee's reference to 'the story of the Divine Creation of man' as taught in the Bible, but there is no doubt that the motivation for the law was the same: to suppress the teaching of a theory which, it was thought, 'denied' the divine creation of man.

8. *Lemon v. Kurtzman*, 403 U.S. 602 (1971), invalidated Pennsylvania and Rhode Island statutes that assisted parochial schools by providing public funds to refurbish buildings and enhance teachers' pay. Even though the laws had a secular purpose of improving educational opportunities of children, an excessive entanglement between church and state was created, and in Rhode Island, the state funds going to teacher salaries had the primary effect of aiding religion. This case produced the primary legal standard that is used today (called "the *Lemon* test) where the public school bears the legal burden to **prove all three of following elements: (1) it had a secular (non-religious) purpose for its action, (2) the action was neutral with regard to**

religion, meaning that it did not advance nor inhibit religion, and (3) the action did not create an excessive governmental entanglement with religion.

9. *Yoder v. Wisconsin*, 406 U.S. 205 (1972), overturned the conviction of an Amishman for refusing to send his children to school beyond the eighth grade. Because Mr. Yoder's decision was based on his fundamental First Amendment right of free exercise of religion, the state of Wisconsin was required to prove that it had a **compelling reason** to apply a criminal penalty for not sending his children to school until they turned sixteen. The Court determined that when two more years of education as required by the state's compulsory attendance law was weighed against the right of the Amish to practice their religion, which also included a form of vocational education in the two years beyond their children's formal schooling, the state's reasons were not sufficiently compelling.

10. *Stone v. Graham*, 449 U.S. 49 (1980), overturned a Kentucky statute mandating the posting of the Ten Commandments in public school classrooms with private dollars because the law's purpose was religious rather than secular.

11. *Meueller v. Allen*, 463 U.S. 388 (1983), upheld a Minnesota statute permitting all taxpayers to deduct educational expenses incurred on behalf of their children for tuition, textbooks, and transportation, even though the law benefited parents of parochial students to a greater degree.

12. *Lynch v. Donnelly*, 465 U.S. 668 (1984), upheld Pawtucket, Rhode Island's display of the nativity scene on private property along with other objects such as a Santa Claus house, a "Seasons Greetings" banner, and a Christmas tree. Said the Court at pages 680-681:

> The City, like the Congresses and Presidents, however, has principally taken note of a significant historical religious event long celebrated in the Western World. The crèche in the display depicts the historical origins of this traditional event long recognized as a National Holiday. . .

The narrow question is whether there is a secular purpose for Pawtucket's display of the crèche. The display is sponsored by the City to celebrate the Holiday and to depict the origins of that Holiday. These are legitimate secular purposes.

13. *Wallace v. Jaffree*, 472 U.S. 38 (1985), struck down an Alabama statute authorizing a daily period of silence in public schools for "meditation or silent prayer." The Court stated at page 60:

The addition of "or voluntary prayer" indicates that the State intended to characterize prayer as a favored practice. Such an endorsement is not consistent with the established principle that the government must pursue a course of complete neutrality toward religion.

14. *Aguilar v. Felton*, 473 U.S. 402 (1985), invalidated New York City's use of federal Title I monies to pay public employees to go into parochial schools and furnish remedial instruction and guidance and clinical services. (This decision was overruled twelve years later in *Agostini v. Felton*, 521 U.S.203 (1997).)

15. *Edwards v. Aguillard*, 482 U.S. 578 (1987), struck down Louisiana's Balanced Treatment for Creation-Science and Evolution-Science in Public School Instruction Act based on the Court having found no secular purpose therefore and determining the law endorsed religion by finding that "the legislative history. . . reveals that the term 'creation science,' as contemplated by the legislature that adopted this Act, embodies the religious belief that a supernatural creator was responsible for the creation of humankind." *Id.* at 591-592.

16. *County of Alleghney v. American Civil Liberties Union*, 492 U.S. 573 (1989), held invalid the Christian Nativity display on the "Grand Staircase" inside the Pittsburgh, Pennsylvania Court House due to the primary effect of advancing or endorsing religion. However, the Court also ruled that no religious advancement occurred by the display on Pittsburgh's public grounds of an 18-foot Chanukah menorah of an "abstract tree-and-branch design" next to a 45-foot Christmas tree beneath which was a sign with the Mayor's name and the inscription, "Salute to Liberty. During this holiday season, the city of Pittsburgh

salutes liberty. Let these festive lights remind us that we are the keepers of the flame of liberty and our legacy of freedom."

In explanation, the Court stated at pages 617-618:

> The tree, moreover, is clearly the predominant element in the city's display. The 45-foot tree occupies the central position beneath the middle archway in front of the Grant Street entrance to the City-County Building; the 18-foot menorah is positioned to one side. Given this configuration, it is much more sensible to interpret the meaning of the menorah in light of the tree, rather than vice versa. In the shadow of the tree, the menorah is readily understood as simply a recognition that Christmas is not the only traditional way of observing the winter-holiday season. In these circumstances, then, the combination of the tree and the menorah communicates, not a simultaneous endorsement of both the Christian and Jewish faiths, but instead, a secular celebration of Christmas coupled with an acknowledgment of Chanukah as a contemporaneous alternative tradition.

17. *Lee v. Weisman*, 505 U.S. 577 (1992), invalidated the practice of a Providence, Rhode Island public school of having an "Invocation" and "Benediction" placed on the graduation agenda with a member of the clergy of Protestant, Catholic, and Jewish faiths conducting the prayers. The Court applied a coercion test to find a violation of the Establishment Clause and stated at pages 595-592 (bold added for emphasis):

> The First Amendment protects speech and religion by quite different mechanisms. Speech is protected by ensuring its full expression even when the government participates, for the very object of some of our most important speech is to persuade the government to adopt an idea as its own. . . The method for protecting freedom of worship and freedom of conscience in religious matters is quite the reverse. **In religious debate or expression the government is not a prime participant**, for the Framers deemed religious establishment antithetical to the freedom of all. The Free Exercise Clause embraces a freedom of conscience and worship that has close parallels in the speech provisions of the First Amendment, but

the **Establishment Clause is a specific prohibition on forms of state intervention in religious affairs** with no precise counterpart in the speech provisions. . . The explanation lies **in the lesson of history that was and is the inspiration for the Establishment Clause, the lesson that in the hands of government what might begin as a tolerant expression of religious views may end in a policy to indoctrinate and coerce.** A state-created orthodoxy puts at grave risk that freedom of belief and conscience which are the sole assurance that religious faith is real, not imposed.

18. *Zobrest v. Catalina Foothills Sch. Dist.*, 509 U.S.1 (1993), ruled that the Establishment Clause was not violated when a sign-language interpreter was provided at public expense to a student of a Catholic school pursuant to the Individual with Disabilities Education Act. The Court stated at page 10:

The service at issue in this case is part of a general government program that distributes benefits neutrally to any child qualifying as "disabled" under the IDEA, without regard to the "sectarian-nonsectarian, or public-nonpublic nature" of the school the child attends. By according parents freedom to select a school of their choice, the statute ensures that a government-paid interpreter will be present in a sectarian school only as a result of the private decision of individual parents. In other words, because the IDEA creates no financial incentive for parents to choose a sectarian school, an interpreter's presence there cannot be attributed to state decisionmaking. . . When the government offers a neutral service on the premises of a sectarian school as part of a general program that "is in no way skewed towards religion, . . . it follows under our prior decisions that provision of that service does not offend the Establishment Clause.

19. *Lamb's Chapel v. Center Moriches Union Free School District*, 508 U.S. 384 (1993), invalidated a New York public school's refusal to allow a church group to lease space for a meeting to show a film on Christian child-rearing and family values. The school's refusal discriminated against the church's freedom of religious expression in that other community groups had been allowed access to the facilities for expressive purposes. Secondly, the Establishment Clause is not

violated by allowing religious groups to have access to public school facilities.

20. *Agostini v. Felton*, 521 U.S.203 (1997), upheld New York City's use of Title I funds to employ public school employees to provide remedial instruction and guidance and clinical services in parochial schools and overturned its 1985 ruling in *Aguilar v. Felton*. The Court stated at pages 224-225:

> As we have repeatedly recognized, government inculcation of religious beliefs has the impermissible effect of advancing religion. Our cases subsequent to *Aquilar* have, however, modified in two significant respects the approach we use to assess indoctrination. First, we have abandoned the presumption . . . that the placement of public employees on parochial school grounds inevitably results in the impermissible effect of state-sponsored indoctrination or constitutes a symbolic union between government and religion. . . [Citing and discussing *Zobrest v. Catalina Foothills School Dist.*, 509 U.S. 1 (1993); see number 17, above.]

> Second, we have departed from the rule relied on in *Ball* that all government aid that directly assists the educational function of religious schools is invalid. In *Witters v. Washington Dept. of Services for the Blind*, 474 U.S. 481, 106 S.Ct. 748, 88 L.Ed.2d 846 (1986), we held that the Establishment Clause did not bar a State from issuing a vocational tuition grant to a blind person who wished to use the grant to attend a Christian college and become a pastor, missionary, or youth director.

21. *Sante Fe Sch. Dist. v. Doe*, 530 U.S. 290 (2000), stuck down a Texas school board policy that allowed students to select a student to give an "invocation and/or message" prior to each home football game based on it (1) being an advancement or endorsement of religion and (2) having a coercive effect on students who do not wish to participate. The Court stated at page 308 (bold added for emphasis):

> In this context the members of the listening audience must perceive the pregame message as a public expression of the views of the majority of the student body delivered with the approval of the

school administration. In cases involving state participation in a religious activity, one of the relevant questions is "**whether an objective observer, acquainted with the text, legislative history, and implementation of the statute, would perceive it as a state endorsement of prayer in public schools.**" . . Regardless of the listener's support for, or objection to, the message, an objective Santa Fe High School student will unquestionably perceive the inevitable pregame prayer as stamped with her school's seal of approval.

In finding that the school's pregame invocation also had an impermissible coercive effect on some student's in attendance, the Court explained at page 312:

Even if we regard every high school student's decision to attend a home football game as purely voluntary, we are nevertheless persuaded that the delivery of a pregame prayer has the improper effect of coercing those present to participate in an act of religious worship. For "the government may no more use social pressure to enforce orthodoxy than it may use more direct means." . . As in *Lee*, "[w]hat to most believers may seem nothing more than a reasonable request that the nonbeliever respect their religious practices, in a school context may appear to the nonbeliever or dissenter to be an attempt to employ the machinery of the State to enforce a religious orthodoxy." . . The constitutional command will not permit the District "to exact religious conformity from a student as the price" of joining her classmates at a varsity football game.

22. *Good News Club v. Milford Central School*, 533 U.S. 98 (2001), struck down a New York school's refusal to allow a Christian children's club to meet after school. The Court considered such refusal to be viewpoint religious discrimination under the First Amendment's free speech clause in that non-religious community groups were allowed to meet for expressive purposes. Secondly, allowing the religious group to meet, as it did nonreligious groups, would not violate the Establishment Clause because it would be a neutral community-use program that does not advance religion. The Court stated at page 114:

[W]e have held that "a significant factor in upholding governmental programs in the face of Establishment Clause attack is their *neutrality* towards religion." . . Milford's implication that granting access to the Club would do damage to the neutrality principle defies logic. For the "guarantee of neutrality is respected, not offended, when the government, following neutral criteria and evenhanded policies, extends benefits to recipients whose ideologies and viewpoints, including religious ones, are broad and diverse." . . The Good News Club seeks nothing more than to be treated neutrally and given access to speak about the same topics as are other groups. Because allowing the Club to speak on school grounds would ensure neutrality, not threaten it, Milford faces an uphill battle in arguing that the Establishment Clause compels it to exclude the Good News Club.

23. *Zelman v. Simmons-Harris*, 536 U.S. 639 (2002), upheld the Ohio Pilot Scholarship Program, a type of voucher plan that gave tuition assistance to parents in the Cleveland City School District with lower income to use to send their children to the public or private school of their choice, including parochial schools. Although the outcome of the program resulted in ninety-six percent of the children attending religious schools, the Court found there to be a secular purpose of promoting educational opportunities for children of poverty, and due to its neutrality, there was not an improper advancement of religion or endorsement thereof. At page 652, the Court gave part of its rationale as follows (bold added for emphasis):

> *Mueller, Witters,* and *Zobrest* thus make clear that where a government aid program is neutral with respect to religion, and **provides assistance directly to a broad class of citizens** who, in turn, **direct government aid to religious schools wholly as a result of their own genuine and independent private choice**, the program is not readily subject to challenge under the Establishment Clause. A program that shares these features **permits government aid to reach religious institutions only by way of the deliberate choices of numerous individual recipients**. The incidental advancement of a religious mission, or the perceived endorsement of a religious message, is **reasonably attributable**

to the individual recipient, not to the government, whose role ends with the disbursement of benefits.

C. The following Indiana statutes pertain to religion in public schools:

1. A parent may make a written request for, and the principal has the discretion to permit (or not permit), the student to attend a school for religious instruction for up to 120 minutes per week. The religious school must keep attendance records and the public school must grant the same attendance credit as if the student were in the public school for the same period of time. See IC 20-33-2-19.

2. Public schools are given the express authority to permit a "voluntary religious observance" provided two statutory provisions are followed: (1) (a) the time for the observance is outside the regular school day (defined as six and one-half hours excluding lunch time), (b) a religious or philosophical group that does not accept voluntary religious observance must be given access to school facilities during the time set for the observance, and (c) the school must provide supervised for recreation and study during such time; and (2) (a) the school and its employees are prohibited from causing or encouraging attendance at the observance, (b) it is insubordination for an employee to so encourage, (c) the school "shall provide written notice to all students and the students' parents" of the religious observance and of the alternative activities for students, (d) the school must ensure that "students do not coerce attendance" at the religious observance and that "no opprobrium attaches among the students or faculty for not participating in the observance, and (e) the school must discontinue the voluntary religious observance if it cannot prevent the "coercion and opprobrium" to students or faculty. See IC 20-30-6, sections 10-12.

3. A parent, or a student of at least age 18, who makes a written objection "to health and hygiene courses because the courses conflict with the student's religious teachings is entitled to be excused from receiving medical instruction or instruction in hygiene or sanitary science without penalties concerning grades or graduation." See IC 20-30-5-9(d).

4. A student whose parent, based on religious grounds, signs a written objection and delivers it to the child's teacher cannot "be required to undergo any testing, examination, immunization, or treatment" required under IC 20-34-3 and IC 20-34-4. Similarly, a teacher with religious grounds who complies with the above-stated written objection requirements cannot be so required. See IC 20-34-3-2. However, a parent with such religious grounds is **not** excused from the duty to furnish the written statement of immunization history required by IC 20-34-4-5.

G

GANGS AND GANG ACTIVITY
(See Chapter Six in the main text.)

Points of Emphasis:

A. Pursuant to IC 35-45-9-1, a "criminal gang" is a group with at least three (3) members that specifically (1) promotes, sponsors, or assists in or participates in, or (2) requires as a condition of membership or continued membership, the commission of a felony or an act that would be a felony if committed by an adult or the offense of battery, which is defined at IC 35-42-2-1 as when a person knowingly or intentionally touches another person in a rude, insolent, or angry manner.

A person who knowingly or intentionally actively participates in a criminal gang commits criminal gang activity, a Class D felony. IC 35-45-9-3.

B. A person who threatens another person because the other person refuses to join a criminal gang or has withdrawn from a criminal gang commits criminal gang intimidation, a Class C felony. IC 35-45-9-4

C. A person who knowingly or intentionally solicits, recruits, entices, or intimidates another individual to join a criminal gang commits criminal gang recruitment, a Class D felony. However, it is a Class C felony if the recruitment, enticement, or intimidation occurs within a thousand feet of school property or the person being solicited, recruited, enticed, or intimidated is less than eighteen years of age. IC 35-45-9-5.

D. Three students who, for example, assist in and/or participate in the offense of battery against another student are by definition a "criminal gang," and subject to conviction if an adult or adjudicated a juvenile delinquent if under age eighteen.

HOMELESS CHILDREN IC 20-50, chapters 1 and 2

A. A "homeless child" for purposes of chapter 1 (appointment of liaison with IDOE) and chapter 2 (tutoring), mirrors the federal definition, and states:

Sec. 1. (a) As used in this chapter, "homeless child" means a minor who lacks a fixed, regular, and adequate nighttime residence.

(b) The term includes:
(1) a child who:
(A) **shares the housing of other persons due to the child's loss of housing, economic hardship, or a similar reason**;
(B) lives in a motel, hotel, or campground due to the lack of alternative adequate accommodations;
(C) lives in an emergency or transitional shelter;
(D) is abandoned in a hospital or other place not intended for general habitation; or
(E) is **awaiting foster care placement**;
2) a child who has a primary nighttime residence that is a public or private place not designed for or ordinarily used as a regular sleeping accommodation for human beings;
(3) a child who lives in a car, a park, a public space, an abandoned building, a bus station, a train station, substandard housing, or a similar setting; and
(4) a child of a migratory worker who lives in circumstances described in subdivisions (1) through (3).

B. Transportation requirements for homeless children appear in this Article below under "TRANSPORTATION."

HOME RULE POWERS (See Chapter One in the main text and BOARDS OF EDUCATION in this Article, above.)

Point of Emphasis:

A. Home rule means that school corporations have, in addition to all statutory powers expressly granted to them, all powers *necessary or desirable* in the conduct their affairs even though the power is not granted by statute of state board of education rule. IC 20-26-3-3(b).

B. Home rule powers may be exercised to the extent that such powers are not expressly prohibited by the Indiana Constitution, statute, or rule of the state board of education. IC 20-26-3-4.

C. Home rule powers are not limitless, however, and must be exercised for the benefit of the public (and not an individual person). See the case of *State v. Poindexter*, 517 N.E.2d 88, (Ind.App. 2 Dist. 1987), where the court ruled that the Town of Wolcott could not use its home-rule authority to authorize its clerk-treasurer to use public funds to pay penalties incurred by her late payment of tax returns. The court stated at page 93:

> Although Poindexter relied upon the Town Board's authorizations permitting her to pay tax penalties and interest from the common fund, the citizens of Wolcott received no benefit as a result of those payments. Rather, Poindexter's nonfeasance in office demonstrated by her delinquent filing of the town's tax returns caused an unnecessary depletion of funds in Wolcott's treasury. Accordingly, the Town Board's authorization to Poindexter did not fall within the spirit and legislative intent of [the Town's home-rule-power statute].

HOME SCHOOLS IC 20-33-2, sections 12, 20, 21 and 28 (See Chapter Eleven in the main text and ATTENDANCE in this Article, above.)

Points of Emphasis:

A. Registration of home schools with the Indiana Department of Education is encouraged, but not legally required.

B. School boards should have a policy for placement of and awarding credits to students who re-enter the public schools from home schools and other nonaccredited private schools.

C. Home school students are permitted to enroll in educational programs or participate in educational initiatives offered by the public school provided the school board or superintendent approves the enrollment. IC 20-33-2-12(b). See *Indiana State Bd. of Educ. v. Brownsburg School Corp.*, 865 N.E.2d 660 (Ind.App. 2007), where the Court of Appeals reversed the State Board of Education and ruled that IC 20-33-2-12(b) authorized the school board or superintendent to deny part-time enrollment to two brothers, one of whom wanted to take band and the other a calculus course and Madrigals. The court also cited the School Corporation Home Rule Act, IC 20-26-3-3, for the school's authority to pass policy allowing only full-time students to enroll or participate in educational programs or initiatives. Lastly, the court rejected the State's argument that Brownsburg School's policy discriminated against part-time students under Article 8, Section 1 of the Indiana Constitution that requires schools to be "equally open to all," by stating at page 668:

> The children were not denied fulltime enrollment at BHS and, therefore, the schools have remained open to all.

D. The Compulsory Attendance Law is violated if parents of nonpublic school students fail to provide "instruction equivalent to that given in the public schools." IC 20-33-2-28.

E. Nonpublic schools are required to keep an accurate daily attendance record for each student and make them available upon the request of the public school superintendent in order to verify enrollment and attendance. IC 20-33-2-20.

IMMUNITY AND OTHER PROTECTION FROM INDIANA TORT CLAIMS (NEGLIGENCE) AND FEDERAL CIVIL RIGHTS ACTIONS (See Chapters One and Two in the main text.)

Points of Emphasis:

A. Immunity from liability in state "tort claim" actions is granted by the Indiana Tort Claims Act, IC 34-13-3-3, which clearly states that a governmental entity (e.g., a public school) and its employees **acting within the scope of their employment** are not liable for a loss from a tort claim or suit that arises under twenty-three listed situations, including:

1. the temporary condition of a public thoroughfare that results from weather (which has been judicially interpreted to include a school's sidewalk and parking lot);

2. the performance of a discretionary function (which means making a general decision, such as deciding to purchase playground equipment, but does not offer protection for the manner in which an administrative act is carried out, such as failing to reasonably inspect and repair the playground equipment);

3. misrepresentation if unintentional (which could arguable apply to such a situation as misinforming a student about applying for a college scholarship that would likely have been received but for the misrepresentation); and

4. injury to a student or the student's property by a school employee as long as the employee was acting reasonably under a discipline policy adopted by the school board.

B. The Tort Claims Act at IC 34-13-2-3 provides the following additional protections to employees of governmental entities:

1. a judgment against the entity or a settlement reached by it prevents a claim against an employee whose conduct resulted in the claim;

2. the entity "shall pay" any court judgment or settlement of a claim or suit against an employee when:

a. the act or omission causing the damages is **within the scope of the employee's employment**; and

b. the governing body makes a determination that paying the judgment or settlement is **in the best interest** of the public body (despite the apparent mandate that the governmental entity "shall pay" damages, a school board, for example, has the discretion not to determine that paying the damages is in its best interests);

3. the entity "shall pay" for all costs and fees incurred by or on behalf of an employee in defending a claim or suit for damages due to the acts or omissions *within the scope of the employee's employment.*

Note that as long as the employee's conduct occurred within the scope of employment, the governmental entity must pay the costs of defense, and not the employee. There is a conflict, however, with the School Powers Act in two respects. First, IC 20-26-5-4(17) requires school boards to make a determination that the employee acted in "good faith" in order to pay for the employee's legal defense. Second, the same statute only permits the school board to hold the employee harmless from damages where the liability was **not** due to the employee's "bad faith" or "malfeasance."

C. Punitive damages against governmental entities and their employees **acting within the scope of employment** are prohibited by Tort Claims Act at IC 34-13-3-4(b).

D. The Tort Claims Act at IC 34-13-3-5, limits lawsuits against a governmental employee **personally** to just five areas where the act or omission of the employee that causes the damages (loss) is:

1. criminal;

2. clearly outside the employee's scope of employment;

3. malicious;

4. willful and wanton; or

5. calculated to benefit the employee personally.

E. Protection against individual or personal civil liability for governmental employees in federal civil rights suits is granted by IC 34-13-4-1, as long as:

1. the loss (damages) occurred due to a noncriminal act or omission of the employee;

2. the act or omission occurred within the scope of employment; **and**

3. the governmental entity defended or had the opportunity to defend the employee.

Where all three conditions are met, the governmental entity must pay (a) any judgment, other than for punitive damages, or (b) any judgment for punitive damages against the employee **if** the entity decides that paying the punitive damages is **in the best interests of the entity**. Lastly, the governmental entity is required to pay all costs and fees incurred by or on behalf of the public employee in a suit brought under the civil rights laws of the United States.

E. The Student Discipline Statute, IC 20-33-8-8(b)(3) gives school personnel "qualified immunity with respect to a disciplinary action taken to promote student conduct ... if the action is taken in **good faith** and is **reasonable.**" This law has been applied to give immunity when teachers have been criminally charged. See *State v. Fettig*, 884 N.E.2d 341 (Ind.App. 2008), rehearing denied, and *Littleton v. State*, 954 N.E. 2d 1070 (Ind.App. 2011).

IMMUNITY GRANTED BY THE JUDICIARY
(See Chapter One of the main text.)

Points of Emphasis:

A. Judicial immunity will be granted state "actors," i.e., public school board members and employees under certain circumstances when suit has been brought under federal civil rights laws, such as section 1983 of the 1871 Civil Rights Act, which allows suits said actors whose actions "under color of state law" are alleged to deprive any citizen or other person of rights granted by the Constitution and laws of the United States.

B. To be granted judicial immunity under a federal section 1983 claim, a public school actor must be able prove **either** (1) the law in question, such as a student's first amendment speech protection, was **not clearly established** at the time of the incident giving rise to the lawsuit, **or** (2) even if the law was clearly established, the particular set of facts to which the law was to be applied were so complex, **a reasonable school actor could not have been certain as how to apply the law**.

1. For the law to be "clearly established" at the time the public school actor must make a decision, it must be found that a reasonable school employee or board member in the shoes of that actor would have had clear guidance from an existing body of legal rulings in order to reach a certain conclusion on how to proceed. See *Porter v. Ascension Parish School Bd.*, 393 F.3d 608 (5th Cir. 2004), where the court granted immunity to the school principal when it determined that the state of First Amendment speech law was not reasonably clear regarding threats in the form of a violent student drawing made at home without any intent to bring it to the attention of anyone at school or elsewhere.

2. The second consideration in granting judicial immunity is the complexity of the given fact situation that the governmental actor faces. The Fifth Circuit Court of Appeals in the *Porter* case, above, noted that "The Supreme Court has observed that, even when a particular legal doctrine is clearly established, '[i]t is sometimes difficult for an [official] to determine how the relevant legal doctrine ... will apply to the factual situation the [official] confronts.'" *Id*. at 620, citing *Saucier v. Katz*, 533 U.S. 194 at 205 (2001).

The Supreme Court in *Saucier*, above, was faced with the issue of whether, in light of the arresting police officers' actions in the use of force to subdue a suspect, they should be granted immunity. The Court stated at 205:

Because "police officers are often forced to make split-second judgments-in circumstances that are tense, uncertain, and rapidly evolving-about the amount of force that is necessary in a particular situation," ... the reasonableness of the officer's belief as to the appropriate level of force should be judged from that on-scene perspective, ... We set out a test that cautioned against the "20/20 vision of hindsight" in favor of deference to the judgment of reasonable officers on the scene... If an officer reasonably, but mistakenly, believed that a suspect was likely to fight back, for instance, the officer would be justified in using more force than in fact was needed.

... The concern of the immunity inquiry is to acknowledge that reasonable mistakes can be made as to the legal constraints on particular police conduct. It is sometimes difficult for an officer to determine how the relevant legal doctrine, here excessive force, will apply to the factual situation the officer confronts. An officer might correctly perceive all of the relevant facts but have a mistaken understanding as to whether a particular amount of force is legal in those circumstances. If the officer's mistake as to what the law requires is reasonable, however, the officer is entitled to the immunity defense.

IMMUNIZATIONS IC 20-34-4, IC20-34-3 (See Chapter Eleven in the main text and FREEDOM OF RELIGION in this Article, above.)

Points of Emphasis:

A. Every child in Indiana is required to be immunized against specifically listed diseases (and additional ones required by the State Department of Health) and a statement of immunization history is required of students to present on the first day of school (with the school being able to waive presentation of proof for only twenty days). Students not in compliance must not be permitted to attend school until such presentation is made. (This action is not to be treated as a suspension or expulsion from school due to the definition of these terms at IC 20-33-8-7 and IC 20-33-8-3, respectively.)

B. Objection to being immunized may be made on religious or documented medical grounds, but the immunization history statement (even if nonexistent) must still be presented on the first day of school (or within twenty days if waived).

C. Schools must notify parents of the immunization requirements.

INTERNET USAGE

Points of Emphasis:

A. School corporations should develop Internet use policies, procedures, and agreements between the school and both the student and the employee. These documents need to detail what is acceptable use and what is the consequence of a violation of the agreement when access is gained through the school's Internet server.

B. The Internet use agreement should also inform the student and employee that there is no expectation of privacy and that access will be monitored in real time or after the fact. Without an expectation of privacy, the Fourth Amendment would not apply to any search by school officials of its own computer system.

C. Private Internet use by students and employees on their own servers and equipment is generally protected by the First and Fourth Amendments, but certain speech like criminal threats are not protected and speech that becomes public is no longer considered private and loses the protection of the Fourth Amendment.

LEAVES OF ABSENCE IC 20-28-10, Federal Family Medical Leave Act (FMLA), Federal Uniformed Services Employment and Reemployment Rights Act (USERRA)

Points of Emphasis:

A. The general rules governing three types of teacher leaves of absence under IC 20-28-10-1 provide:

1. School corporations may grant teacher leaves not to exceed one year for a sabbatical, disability, or sickness; however, a school may grant consecutive leaves.

2. Schools are allowed to grant partial compensation for a leave "in an amount the school corporation determines." The original language was adopted prior to the Collective Bargaining Law; so, since January 1, 1974, schools have had the duty to bargain the partial compensation for leaves with the exclusive representative of teachers.

3. Leaves for teachers who are pregnant must be granted and are governed by the language in the section dealing with pregnancy leaves.

4. The teacher and the school corporation are required to sign a regular teacher's contract for each school year in which any part of the leave is granted.

B. Other conditions pertaining to leaves are provided in IC 20-28-10-2 as follows:

1. Existing rights of a teacher at the time the leave starts remain intact, specifically professional and established teacher status; accumulated years of successive service; service performed under a teacher's per IC 20-28-6-8; and status or rights negotiated under the Collective Bargaining Law.

2. During the leave the teacher can maintain coverage in a group insurance plan by paying the total premium including the school's share, but all or part of the costs of the premium may be paid by the school if negotiated.

3. During leave extending into part of a school year, sick days may be accumulated by the teacher **but only** in proportion to a formula that divides the total number of days the teacher on leave is paid by the total number of teacher days to be worked. For example, if the teacher on leave is paid for eighteen days in a one-hundred-and-eighty-day school year, the teacher would accumulate one-tenth of the sick days called for in the collective bargaining agreement.

4. During a probationary teacher's leave, the probationary years of service needed to become a professional or established teacher is uninterrupted, but if the entire year is spent on leave, it does not count as a year toward achieving professional or established teacher status.

5. All or part of a leave granted for sickness or disability (including a pregnancy-related disability) may be used by the teacher as paid sick days. **However**, the teacher is **not entitled to paid sick days** when the teacher is able to perform the teacher's regular duties as certified by the teacher's doctor. The statute states that in this instance, "the teacher is entitled to complete the remaining leave without pay." IC 20-28-10-2(e).

C. A sabbatical leave is for improvement of professional skills through (1) advanced study, (2) work experience, (3) teacher exchange programs, or (4) approved educational travel. The statute requires the teacher upon return from the leave to work the same length of time as the sabbatical leave. IC 20-28-10-3.

D. A school corporation may place a teacher on disability or sick leave not to exceed one year without written request or consent: however, a "teacher placed on a disability or sick leave without a written request is entitled to a hearing on that action under IC 20-28-7.5." IC 20-28-10-4.

E. A pregnant teacher is given the following rights by IC 20-28-10-5:

1. ability to work as long into the pregnancy as she wants if able to perform the job;

2. the grant of a leave any time between the start of pregnancy and one year following the birth of the child, **provided that** she notifies the superintendent at least thirty days before the date on which the leave is to start; the teacher must also notify the superintendent of the expected length of the leave and provide either the doctor's certification of pregnancy or copy of the birth certificate, whichever is applicable. (The teacher, if a shorter leave was requested, can ask for a second maternity leave within the one-year-following-the-child's-birth period according to the Court of Appeals in the case *of Board of Sch. Trustees*

of Salem Comm. Sch. Corp. v. Robertson, 637 N.E.2d 181 (Ind.App. 1994.) An exception in case of an emergency is provided; and

3. ability to use paid sick days during the temporary disability portion of the pregnancy leave, **but** the teacher is not allowed to use sick days after the disability period is over as indicated by her doctor, and can complete the remaining days of the leave without pay; **however**, the teacher may be compensated for leave days when not disabled if the collective bargaining agreement so provides.

For example, if a teacher delivered her child on April 16 and was granted a leave from April 2 until one year from the birth of her child, and her doctor indicated that she was under a medical disability from April 2 until May 29, the last day of school, the teacher could use accumulated sick days between April 2 and May 29, but could not use remaining sick days when school started on August 16. She could then take the remainder of the leave without pay.

F. Teacher leaves for military service are governed by IC 20-28-10, sections 6 through 11. Generally speaking, these provisions grant protections that preserve their status and contract rights during the service as if they had not gone on leave. Section 9 grants the right to salary increases during the time spent on military leave when it says "All rights to changes of salary or position . . . accrue to the teacher as if no interruption occurred." Although the leave is without pay, a teacher on leave would receive a year's bump on the salary schedule.

G. The federal Uniformed Services Employment and Reemployment Rights Act (USERRA), 38 U.S.C. [United State Code] sections 4301 *et seq.* prohibits discrimination against members of the United States military or its reserve forces, and like Indiana's law, preserves status and contract rights, and requires reinstatement with certain conditions. Also, the returning employee, teacher or non-teacher, has the right to resume with any increase in salary that would have occurred had they remained working.

H. Family Medical Leave Act (FMLA)

1. An employer, private or governmental, of fifty or more employees

must grant medical-related leaves involving a **"serious medical condition"** to an "eligible" employee, which is defined to mean one who has been employed with the employer a minimum of 1,250 hours during a twelve-month period before the leave begins.

a. It is the employer's burden to maintain records that show the employee's hours are below 1,250 in order to deny eligibility.

b. A full-time teacher is eligible even if 1,250 hours have not been worked in the preceding twelve-month period.

c. The employer is required to give written notice to the employee who requests FMLA leave **within two business days** if the employee is **not eligible**; failure to do so makes the employee eligible.

d. If a husband and wife work for the same employer, they are limited to a combined total of twelve weeks for a child's birth or adoption, or for a parent's care who has a serious health condition.

2. According to the U.S. Department of Labor (DOL), "a **serious health condition** means an illness, injury, impairment, or physical or mental condition involving:

a. any period of incapacity or treatment connected with inpatient care (i.e., an overnight stay) in a hospital, hospice, or residential medical care facility;

b. a period of incapacity requiring absence of more than three calendar days from work, school, or other regular daily activities that also involves continuing treatment by (or under the supervision of) a health care provider;

c. any period of incapacity due to pregnancy, or for prenatal care;

d. any period of incapacity (or treatment therefore) due to a chronic serious health condition   (e.g., asthma, diabetes, epilepsy, etc.);

e. a period of incapacity that is permanent or long-term due to a condition for which treatment may not be effective (e.g., Alzheimer's, stroke, terminal disease, etc.); or

f. any absences to receive multiple treatments (including any period of recovery that follows) by, or on referral by, a health care provider for a condition that likely would result in incapacity of more than three consecutive days if left untreated (e.g., chemotherapy, physical therapy, dialysis, etc.)." www.dol.gov/elaws/esa/fmla

3. The DOL states:

"Leave taken to care for a spouse, son, daughter or parent with a serious health condition may be taken a few hours at a time (for example to keep a doctor's appointment for treatment or to keep an appointment for physical therapy) (intermittent leave) or on a part-time basis (for example one parent provides care for a child one half of the day each day of the week, and the other parent provides care the other half day) (reduced leave schedule) when the leave is necessary for planned and/or unanticipated medical treatment by or under the supervision of a health care provider." www.dol.gov/elaws/esa/fmla

4. According to the DOL: "There are four methods for determining the 12-month period in which the 12 weeks of leave entitlement occurs. The employer has the option of selecting any one, but once selected, it must be applied uniformly. Below is a list of the four methods:

  1. Calendar year

  2. Fixed 12-month "leave year" such as fiscal year, a year required by state law, or a year starting on an employee's "anniversary" date

  3. 12-month period measured forward from the date any employee's first FMLA leave begins

  4. "Rolling" 12-month period measured backward from the date an employee uses any FMLA leave An employer wishing to change to another alternative is required to give at least 60 days notice to all employees." www.dol.gov/elaws/esa/fmla

5. The twelve-week FMLA leave is without pay, but the employee may use paid sick leave days if available. The employer is required to continue benefits, including health insurance, during the leave, but the employee continues to pay the employee's share of the premiums.

6. When an FMLA leave is foreseeable (e.g., surgery), the employee must give at least a thirty-day advance notice to the employer and the employer has the right to require certification from a doctor when the reason for leave is a serious health condition of the employee or an immediate family member. For leave requests that are not foreseeable, the employee is to notify the employer as soon as practicable.

7. If intermittent leave is necessary in such circumstances as the employee's illness requiring scheduled medical treatments or to care for an immediate family member, the employee must attempt to schedule the absences in order to not unreasonably disrupt the employer's business.

8. The employer is obligated, under possible penalty of $100 for every willful offense, to post a notice to all employee approved by the Secretary of Labor that explains the provisions of FMLA. Failure to post the notice also prevents the employer from taking any adverse action against the employee who, for example, does not provide sufficient notice of taking the leave.

9. The employer must notify an employee who requests FMLA leave as soon as practicable (two business days) of the employee's eligibility.

10. According to the Department of Labor: "There are eight pieces of information that an employer must provide in writing to an employee who requests FMLA leave:

1. Whether the leave will be counted against the employee's FMLA leave entitlement;

2. Requirements for furnishing medical certification (Form WH-380) for a serious health condition and the consequences for failing to do so;

3. The employee's right to substitute paid leave and whether the employer will require the substitution of paid leave;

4. Requirements for making any health benefit premium payments; consequences for failing to make timely payments; and, circumstances under which coverage might lapse;

5. Requirements to submit a fitness-for-duty certificate to be restored to employment;

6. Employee's status as a "key" employee;

7. Employee's right to restoration when leave is completed; and

8. Employee's potential liability if the employer makes the employee's health insurance premium payments while the employee is on unpaid FMLA leave if the employee fails to return to work." www. dol.gov/elaws/esa/fmla

11. The Department of Labor provides the following notice:

The Family and Medical Leave Act was amended on January 28, 2008. The Act now permits a "spouse, son, daughter, parent, or next of kin" to take up to 26 workweeks of leave to care for a "member of the Armed Forces, including a member of the National Guard or Reserves, who is undergoing medical treatment, recuperation, or therapy, is otherwise in outpatient status, or is otherwise on the temporary disability retired list, for a serious injury or illness." www.dol.gov/elaws/esa/fmla

12. Complaints of a violation of the FMLA are investigated by the Wage and Hour Division of the DOL. If a violation is determined and a mutual settlement cannot be achieved, the DOL may sue in federal court to obtain compliance. The FMLA also allows an employee to bring suit for an alleged violation of FMLA by the employer.

LEGAL SETTLEMENT LAW IC 20-26-11

Points of Emphasis:

A. The statutory rules for determining the legal settlement of a student in order to establish where the student is entitled to attend school without the payment of "transfer tuition" are found at IC 20-26-11-2, which contains the following seven basic rules:

1. The first enumerated rule is that the legal settlement of a student (who is not emancipated) is in the attendance area of the school corporation where the student's **parents reside**.

a. The term "reside" or "residence" is defined to mean "a permanent and principal habitation that an individual uses for a home for a fixed or indefinite period, at which the individual remains when not called elsewhere for work, studies, recreation, or other temporary or special purposes." IC 20-26-11-1.

b. If a court order grants a person custody of student, the residence of the student is where that person resides (except for section (2)(3) of the statute that is explained in subdivision D., below).

2. The second enumerated rule applies to the situation where the student's mother and father are divorced or separated; it declares that the legal settlement of the student is the school corporation whose attendance area contains the **residence of the parent with whom the student is living**, but only in the following situations where:

a. no court order has been made establishing the custody of the student;

b. both parents have agreed on the parent or person with whom the student will live; or

c. the parent granted custody has abandoned the student.

However, in the event of a dispute between the parents, or between the parents and the student who is at least age eighteen, the legal settlement must be determined as otherwise provided in IC 20-26-11-2.

3. The third enumerated rule creates an **election procedure when divorced or separated parents live in different school corporations**; it allows the **custodial parent** (or student who is at least age eighteen) **by at least fourteen days before the first**

student day of the school year to elect to attend school tuition free in the school corporation **of either parent's residence** regardless of where the student lives.

If this election is not made within the required fourteen days, legal settlement is to be the school corporation containing the residence of the **parent granted physical custody by court order**.

4. The fourth enumerated rule applies if the legal settlement of the student "**cannot reasonably be determined** *and* **the student is being supported by, cared for by, and living with some other individual**; if this situation exists, legal settlement is declared to be in **the attendance area of that individual's residence**, *but not if* the parents of the student are able to support the student and have made the placement or allowed the student to live with the other individual primarily for the purpose of attending school in the corporation of the other individual's residence.

a. Under the fourth rule, if the facts are in dispute, the school corporation where this other individual resides is granted the authority to condition acceptance of the student's legal settlement on the appointment of that individual as the legal guardian or custodian of the student.

b. Also under the fourth rule, is a **follow-up rule**, i.e., if the facts demonstrate that (a) the student does not live with the parents because they are unable to support the student, **and** (b) the student is not living with the individual in the other school corporation primarily to attend that school, the student's legal settlement is **where the student resides** (and the establishment of a legal guardianship cannot be required by the school corporation where the student resides).

c. Lastly, under the fourth rule, it is stated that if a legal guardianship or custodianship is established "**solely to attend school in a particular school corporation**," such establishment "**does not affect the determination of legal settlement** of the student" under the Legal Settlement Law. In other words, the school may legally ignore the court order in deciding legal settlement.

5. The fifth enumerated rule applies where the **student is married** and living with a spouse; it establishes legal settlement in the school corporation **where the student and spouse reside.**

6. The sixth enumerated rule applies in the case of a student whose parents are living outside the United States for educational pursuits or employment, maintain no permanent home in any school district in the United States, and have placed the student in the home of another person; it establishes legal settlement of the student in the attendance area where the other person resides.

7. The seventh enumerated rule applies when the **student is emancipated**, and establishes legal settlement in the school corporation of the emancipated student's residence.

a. Indiana Code 20-26-11-4 states that "a student is emancipated when the student: (1) furnishes the student's support from the student's own resources; (2) is not dependent in any material way on the student's parents for support; (3) files or is required by applicable law to file a separate tax return; and (4) maintains a residence separate from that of the student's parents."

b. It is advisable to have a student who claims emancipation to furnish an affidavit signed under penalty of perjury stating facts that support all four of the statutory conditions. (It is wise to require the student to provide additional supportive documentation such as paycheck stubs and receipts for rent, utility, and car payments, including insurance.)

B. Another legal settlement rule that was passed in 2008 (but not enumerated in IC 20-26-11-2) applies to a student whose parents **move to an adjacent school corporation** after having maintained legal settlement in the original school corporation for at least two consecutive years immediately before moving. This rule **permits the student to continue attending the original school** without the payment of "cash tuition," **but only if** both principals and both superintendents of the affected schools jointly agree. Further, the decision to stay at the original school may not be based "primarily on athletic reasons," and the parents have to provide the student's transportation. IC 20-26-11-30.

C. If the legal settlement of the student changes after the student has begun attending school in any given school year, the student may complete the current semester at that school corporation. If the change occurred in the first semester and the student elects to complete that semester, the school has the discretion to allow the student to complete the school year without tuition payments.

D. The Department of Education is directed to prepare the forms of agreement to be used in the situations described in subsections C., D., E., and G. above. These forms are available at its website: http://www.doe.in.gov/legal/pdf/custodial_statement_instructions.pdf

E. The State Board of Education is given the authority to hear all disputes, "upon timely application of any interested party," that apply to legal settlement, the amount of tuition, the right to transfer or attend any school corporation, and any other matter contained in the legal settlement chapter of the law. It also is to hear all appeals arising under the chapter and from an expulsion of a student for lack of legal settlement. IC 20-26-11-15.

F. Generally, as to student transfers because of better accommodation due to crowded conditions or, at the high school level, due to curriculum offerings "that are important to the vocational or academic aspirations of the student," if either the "transferor" or "transferee" school denies the request (which by State Board rule must be made by April 1 of the preceding school year), appeal may be made to the State Board for its determination. IC 20-26-11-5.

1. Note that in the State Board's rule at 511 IAC 1-6-3 on "better accommodation" two other reasons for transfer that are not contained in IC 20-26-11-5 are allowed: (1) risk of illness at the transferor school, and (2) the transferor school attended by the student is not fully accredited.

2. Because the April 1 deadline for requests to transfer under the State Board rule applies to crowded conditions and high school curriculum

offerings, there is no stated deadline for requests based on risk of illness and lack of full accreditation.

G. Schools have the option of either requiring the payment of what are known as "cash transfers" (when the receiving school agrees to accept the enrollment of the student whose parents reside in another corporation and are willing to pay the statutory calculated amount of transfer), **or** the school board may decide **not to charge any** tuition. IC 20-26-11-6.

1. If transfer tuition is charged, the parent must pay the transfer amount calculated in the formula contained at IC 20-26-11-13.

2. It is highly advisable for those that accept transfer students (whether transfer is charged or not) to develop a policy or administrative rules that list neutral, non-discriminatory, criteria that will be used to evaluate which students will be accepted and which will not. Examples of such criteria are academic achievement, good discipline record, extracurricular participation (including clubs), and school and community activities and leadership. No discrimination may be made on the basis of classifications protected by the state and federal constitutions or statutes prohibiting discrimination based on race, color, national origin, alienage, religion, gender, or disability. Also, note that Title IX's regulations prohibit discrimination based on marital status and pregnancy.

LICENSURE   IC 20-28-2, IC 20-28-5, and 515 IAC 1-1-1 *et seq.* (See Chapter Four in the main text.)

Points of Emphasis:

A. The Indiana Department of Education (IDOE) is given the legal responsibility for the licensing of teachers by IC 20-28-2-1, subject only to the state Board of Education's rule making authority under IC 20-28-2-6.

Any reference to 515 IAC (Indiana Administrative Code) will be to the licensing rules of the State Board of Education.

B. School corporations "shall employ only teachers, administrators, and student services specialists properly licensed" under rules of the State Board. 511 IAC 6.1-6-1.

C. **Definition of "License"** per IC 20-28-1-7, states:

"License" refers to a document issued by the department that grants permission to serve as a particular kind of teacher. The term includes any certificate or permit issued by the department.

D. **Definition of "teacher"** per 20-18-2-22, states:

(a) "Teacher" means a professional person whose position in a school corporation requires certain educational preparation and licensing **and whose primary responsibility is the instruction of students.**

(b) For purposes of IC 20-28, the term includes the following:
  (1) A superintendent.
  (2) A principal.
  (3) A teacher.
  (4) A librarian.

According to the Indiana Court of Appeals in the case of *Switzerland County Sch. Corp. v. Sartori*, 442 N.E.2d 702 (Ind.App. 1982), "the contract involved herein was illegal, [and] hence void as a matter of law. . . ." *Id.* at 703. The contract in issue was a Regular Teacher's Contract entered into by the school corporation and Sartori, a person without a teacher's license who was assigned to teach vocational-agriculture. In ruling that the school's dismissal of Sartori before the end of the school year was not a breach of contract, the court stated at page 704:

Additionally, the public policy considerations underlying the earlier legislative mandate that public school teachers be licensed are as valid today as they were a century ago. Perhaps the best articulation of this concern was expressed in the case of *Jackson School Township v. Farlow*, (1881) 75 Ind. 118, . . . where our supreme court held that even though a person may have the necessary learning, ability, and preparation for the duties of a teacher, unless he were also properly licensed he could not recover damages for breach of a contract entered into with officers of a public school corporation. Judge Elliott, in writing for the court, said,

> "The purpose of the statute is to compel those who desire to enter upon the responsible duties of teachers to submit to an examination by competent school officers, and to effect this purpose the stringent provision prohibiting recoveries by unlicensed teachers was incorporated. The question of qualification and preparation must be determined by the school authorities, not by courts or juries."

75 Ind. at 119-120. Likewise, current legislation evinces no intent that the matters of teacher qualification and licensing be left to courts and juries.

E. All applicants for a teacher's license must submit a limited criminal history and the IDOE cannot issue a license unless the applicant has demonstrated proficiency on a written exam in the areas of basic reading, writing, mathematics, pedagogy, and knowledge of content area. If the applicant is seeking administrative or director licensure, leadership proficiency must be demonstrated on a written exam.

F. **License suspension or revocation** is under the jurisdiction of the IDOE per IC 20-28-5-7 and the rule of the State Board at 515 IAC 9-1-18; due process procedures contained in said rule must be followed and the revocation or suspension of license must have the written recommendation of the superintendent of public instruction.

1. Although the Legislature states at IC 20-28-5-8(c) that the IDOE must **permanently revoke** the license of a person who is known to have been convicted of a felony for 30 listed crimes, the IDOE rule makes no mention of permanent revocation and states that a person whose license has been revoked may petition the IDOE for license reinstatement at any time after the passage of three years. 515 IAC 9-1-18(e). (The statute would prevail over the rule and, therefore, the IDOE would be prevented from reinstating a permanently revoked license).

a. The burden is placed on the applicant for license reinstatement (from a revocation or suspension) to prove at a "fitness hearing" that the person is fit to hold a license.

b. The State Board is required to consider seven listed factors in its consideration of the reinstatement petition.

2. The IDOE under statute and its rules, following the due process hearing (which can be conducted by an administrative law judge appointed by it), may also revoke or suspend a teaching license for immorality, misconduct in office, incompetency, or willful neglect of duty.

G. **Emergency permits** are governed by 515 IAC 9-1-19 whereby the "applicant" (defined at 515 IAC 1-1-96(2) as "the person or entity that applies for the licenses and permits granted by the board or department under a certain rule") must apply between July 1 and April 15 of the school year for which the permit is sought, but no later than 12 weeks after the applicant begins service. 1. The application must contain documentation from the school superintendent "certifying an emergency need for the applicant in the content or areas or the school setting or settings of the request."

2. The emergency permits "may be renewed at the request of the employing school superintendent" up to two times, but for each renewal, there must be evidence of completion of six-semester-hours relevant course work or verification of "appropriate progress" by the licensing advisor of the college or university.

3. It appears that applicants for these permits may include persons seeking all certificated positions including administrators, except for the superintendent (which is covered by another rule at 515 IAC 8-1-50).

H. **Temporary superintendent licenses** are governed by 515 IAC 8-1-50, which requires the school board to submit the request to the "temporary superintendent license approval committee."

1. The applicant must have a "masters degree or higher from an institution of higher learning approved by the board" (meaning the State Board of Education).

2. If granted, the license is valid until the "termination or expiration of the applicant's contract with the governing body." Hence, if another school board hires this person as its superintendent, it, like the first board, must seek a temporary license for him/her.)

I. The **substitute teacher permit rule** at 515 IAC 5-1 provides:

1. "The permit is a renewable three-year license issued to a teacher upon application from the Indiana school district superintendent as defined by the Indiana school district substitute plan...."

2. The substitute plan of the school district must include five listed criteria: (1) the school district's requirements for a substitute permit; (2) the minimum of a high school diploma earned from an accredited school; (3) a plan for reciprocity with other Indiana school districts; (4) training and mentoring procedures for first-year substitutes; and (5) additional documentation required by the IDOE.

3. The current substitute plan must be on file with the IDOE.

4. Schools are prohibited from employing substitutes with permits when licensed teachers are available to substitute.

5. Substitutes who hold a valid Indiana professional, provisional, standard, or reciprocal license may substitute an unlimited number of days.

6. Substitutes holding a valid Indiana provisional, professional, or standard license who serve in the same teaching position "for more than fifteen (15) successive days" must be compensated on the regular pay scale for teachers in the school corporation (but do not have to be given a written contract). IC 20-28-9-7(b) and IC 20-28-6-4(a).

J. The **Transition to Teaching Program** is created by IC 20-28-4-1 in order to "facilitate the transition into the teaching profession of competent professionals in fields other than teaching" and to "allow competent professionals who do not hold a teaching license to earn and be issues a teaching license through participation in and satisfactory completion of the program." The State Board of

Education rule appears at 515 IAC 1-6.

K. The **Beginning Teacher Residency Program rule** is governed by 515 IAC 1-5-3.

L. The **Beginning Building Level Administrator Residency rule** is found at 515 IAC 1-5-3.1.

M-N

MEDICAL AND HEALTH RELATED IC 20-34-3, IC 20-33-8-13, IC 20-34-5, IC 34-30-14, 511 IAC 7-36-9 and 7-42-12

Points of Emphasis:

A. A student who is ill, has a communicable disease, or is infested with parasites may be sent home by the principal with a note to the parent describing the problem, and recommending that a physician be consulted. IC 20-34-3-9. (This action is not to be treated as a disciplinary suspension or expulsion per the definition of these terms at IC 20-33-8-7 and IC 20-33-8-3, respectively.)

1. A public health care facility must provide the medical care if the parents cannot afford to pay. If no such facility exits, the township trustee or other appropriate governmental agency must provide the care.

2. Re-admission of the student to school is permissible when it is apparent to school officials that the condition is no longer present or upon certification of health by a physician or Christian Science practitioner.

B. Testing of students for sickle cell anemia, lead poisoning, vision, and hearing is addressed at IC 20-34-3-10 through 15.

C. Medications that are kept by the school to administer to students may (1) be released to the parents or a student at least age 18 with written consent of the parent or (2) sent home with any student if the parent gives written permission. IC 20-34-3-18.

D. Students may self-possess and administer medications at school with annual written authorization of the parent and a doctor's statement that (1) the student has an acute or chronic disease for which the medicine has been prescribed and (2) the student has been instructed on administration procedures; notice of this right must appear in the student discipline rules. IC 20-33-8-13.

E. State Board of Education rules requiring a school board policy and procedures for administering medications are found at 511 IAC 7-36-9.

F. Statutory immunity for school personnel administering medication, provided certain conditions are followed, is found at IC 34-30-14.

G. The care and treatment of students with diabetes including development of a treatment plan for each student, training of personnel, and seeking volunteers is found at IC 20-34-5.

H. The homebound instruction rule for students with injuries and temporary or chronic illnesses is found at 511 IAC 7-42-12, and reads as follows:

> Sec. 12. (a) All students with injuries and temporary or chronic illnesses that preclude their attendance in school, including students who are not eligible for special education and related services, must be provided with instruction.
>
> (b) Before instruction for a student unable to attend school can begin, the parent must provide the school corporation with a written statement from a physician (which includes a doctor of osteopathy) with a valid, unlimited license to practice medicine, or a Christian Science practitioner, that states one (1) of the following:
>
> (1) The student has a temporary illness or injury that will require the student's absence from school for a minimum of twenty (20) consecutive instructional days. If the:
>
> (A) illness or injury occurs less than twenty (20) instructional days prior to the end of the school year; and

(B) student needs instruction to meet promotion or graduation requirements;

the physician's statement must indicate that the student will be unable to attend school through the end of the current school year.

(2) The student has a chronic illness or other medical condition that will require the student's absence for an aggregate of at least twenty (20) instructional days over the period of the school year.... [Remainder omitted.]

NEGLIGENCE IC 34-13-3-4 and IC 34-13-4-1
(See Chapter Two in the main text and IMMUNITY FROM TORT ACTIONS in this Article, above.)

Points of Emphasis:

A. The tort of negligence is not established by a legislature, but is created and defined by the judicial system through case (or common) law. It is generally described as a person's breach of a legal duty of care by an act or omission that fails to exercise reasonable or ordinary care, and that directly results in injury to another person. See the Indiana Supreme Court's landmark case of *Miller v. Griesel, 308 N.E.2d 701* (Ind. 1974), which ruled that the school principal's and teacher's actions did not rise to the level of a failure to use reasonable care, even though a fifth grade student lost the sight of an eye when a dynamite blasting cap exploded when the teacher was out of the room.

1. In the context of a public (or private) school, the non-criminal conduct of a teacher or other employee with a legal duty of care whose act or omission that causes injury is within the employee's scope of employment is imputed to the employer by the doctrine of *respondeat superior*. This means that the superior entity must respond in damages to the injured party and not the employee.

2. For employees of governmental employers such as public schools, the Indiana Tort Claims Act at IC 34-13-3 grants immunity and protection against the payment of damages as long as the act causing

the injury occurs within the scope of employment and is not criminal, malicious, willful or wanton, or designed to benefit the employee personally.

3. The Tort Claims Act also limits the maximum amount of damages that a governmental employer must pay for injury or death to one person per negligent occurrence to $700,000; and for such injury or death to all persons in one occurrence to $5,000,000.

B. School administrators, teachers, aides, bus drivers, and other personnel who supervise students have a legal duty to use reasonable care in providing a safe environment to protect children from harm.

C. Schools have two common law complete defenses to a claim of negligence: (1) contributory negligence by the injured party who reasonably should have foreseen that his/her act or omission would have resulted in harm, and (2) assumption of a risk by the injured party who knew of the danger involved and undertook the action regardless of the known danger.

D. A parent, or other volunteer, who is assisting the school corporation in an activity sponsored by the school corporation is considered an employee for purposes of a negligence suit, and possess the same protections against personal liability as paid school employees.

E. School corporations need to carry sufficient liability insurance for protection in the event of a lawsuit and eventual damages caused by the negligent actions of their employees and volunteers.

F. A comprehensive risk management program should be adopted by the school board to minimize injuries and claims of negligence.

OPEN DOOR LAW IC 5-14-1.5

Points of Emphasis:

A. The legislatively declared purpose of the Indiana Open Door Law (ODL) is stated at IC 5-14-1.5-1:

In enacting this chapter, the general assembly finds and declares that this state and its political subdivisions exist only to aid in the conduct of the business of the people of this state. It is the intent of this chapter that the official action of public agencies be conducted and taken openly, unless otherwise expressly provided by statute, in order that the people may be fully informed. The purposes of this chapter are remedial, and its provisions are to be liberally construed with the view of carrying out its policy.

B. The following important definitions appear in the ODL (IC 5-14-1.5-2):

1. **"Public agency"** is broadly defined to mean:

a. a school corporation or other entity, by whatever name designated, exercising in a limited geographical area the executive, administrative, or legislative power of the state or a delegated local governmental power.

b. any entity which is subject to budget review by either the department of local government finance or the governing body of a county, city, town, township, or school corporation, or an audit by the state board of accounts that is required by statute, rule, or regulation.

c. any building corporation of a political subdivision of the state of Indiana that issues bonds for the purpose of constructing public facilities.

d. any advisory commission, committee, or body created by statute, ordinance, or executive order to advise the governing body of a public agency. (Building-level school improvement committees are public agencies subject to the ODL since they were created by statute to advise public school boards.)

2. **"Governing body"** means two or more individuals who are the board or other body of a public agency which takes **official action** upon public business, or **any committee appointed directly by the governing body or its presiding officer** to which authority to take official action upon public business has been delegated.

a. It is important to note that a committee **appointed by the superintendent or other administrator**, is **not a "governing body"** subject to the requirements of the ODL, unless, of course, some of the administrative committee's membership included a **majority of school board members**. (The Indiana Court of Appeals in *Robinson v. Indiana University*, 638 N.E.2d (435 (Ind.App. 1994), held that the ODL does not apply to committees that are not directly appointed by the governing body or its president.)

b. This definition clearly states that a school board's appointed "agent or agents" for collective bargaining purposes is **not a "governing body"** that would subject the appointed person or persons to the ODL's requirements.

3. **"Meeting"** means a **gathering of a majority of the governing body** of a public agency for the purpose of taking **official action** upon **public business**.

a. Excluded from the definition of "meeting" are:

(1) any **social or chance gathering not intended to avoid** the ODL;

(2) any **on-site inspection** of any project or program;

(3) traveling to and attending meetings of organizations devoted to betterment of government;

(4) a gathering to discuss an industrial or a commercial prospect that does not include a conclusion as to recommendations, policy, decisions, or final action on the terms of a request or an offer of public financial resources;

(5) an orientation of members of the governing body on their role and responsibilities as public officials, but not for any other official action; or

(6) a gathering for the sole purpose of administering an oath of office to an individual.

b. These exclusions mean, for example, that a social gathering with the entire school board in attendance, such as a cook0out, is exempt from the ODL's requirements as long as there is no evidence of an intent to circumvent the law and, of course, a majority of the school board members do not happen to discuss at the same moment any matter of school business during the social occasion.

4. **"Official action"** means where the school board would do any one or more of the following:

a. receive information (i.e., sit and listen to someone speak on a matter of public business);

b. deliberate;

c. make recommendations;

d. establish policy;

e. make decisions; or

f. take final action.

Note that the phrase "make decisions" is separate from "take final action," the latter of which is defined as "a vote." This is important later in the ODL's executive session provision, which only prohibits a school board from taking "final action," i.e., a vote, in executive session, but does not prohibit making decisions therein.

5. **"Public business"** is broadly defined to mean any function upon which the school board is empowered or authorized to take official action.

6. **"Executive session"** means a meeting from which the public is excluded, except the governing body may admit those persons necessary to carry out its purpose.

7. **"Final action"** means **a vote** by a school board on any motion, proposal, resolution, rule, or regulation.

8. **"Deliberate"** means a discussion which may reasonably be expected to result in official action.

C. Section three of the ODL (IC 5-14-1.5-3) states the following rules:

1. All meeting of a governing body, except for executive sessions, "must be open at all times for the purpose of permitting members of the public to observe and record them."

2. Secret ballot votes are expressly prohibited.

3. A member of the governing body who is not physically in attendance at a meeting may participate by telephone or other electronic means, but cannot vote or be considered present at the meeting unless it is expressly allowed by another statute. (Nothing in the Education Code permits such.)

4. Meeting memoranda when a physically-absent member participates electronically must state those who were physically present, those who participated electronically, and those who were totally absent.

D. The **"series of gatherings"** prohibition is contained at IC 5-14-1.5-3.1, which states that a governing body member is considered present at a gathering (in addition to being physically there) if participation is by telephone or other electronic means, excluding, however, e-mail participation.

1. As applied to a public school board, the ODL would be violated **only if**:

a. more than one gathering of less than a majority of individual members occurred within a seven-consecutive-day period;

b. the sum of the different members that gathered totaled at least a quorum of the board;

c. the multiple gatherings concerned the same subject matter and involved the taking of "official action" on "public business;" and

d. **one of the gatherings was attended by three members, who were less than a quorum**, and the other gatherings had at least two members present.

2. The critical provision in bold language under "d," immediately above, means that only those school boards with six or more members could ever violate this prohibition, and thus these six-or-greater boards could not possibly violate it if no more than two members at a time gathered to take official action on public business.

For example, if on a seven-person board, members A and B discussed dismissing a coach at bridge on Saturday night, members C and D discussed the same thing at church on Sunday, E and F, considered the same subject on the golf course Sunday, and F and G the same on the telephone Sunday night, the board could, without violating the ODL, fire the coach at a validly called and held meeting on Monday night.

3. Expressly excluded from the series-of-gatherings violation (in addition to the social/chance gathering, onsite inspections, travel to an from certain meetings, board-member orientation regarding their role as public officials, and gathering for the sole purpose of administering the oath of office to a board member) is the following gathering contained at IC 5-14-1.5-3.1(c)(8) (bold added for emphasis):

> a gathering between **less than a quorum** of the members of the governing body **intended solely for members to receive information and deliberate on whether a member or members may be inclined to support a member's proposal or a particular piece of legislation** and at which no other official action will occur.

E. If a school board uses an agenda (no law requires such), the agenda must be posted at the building entrance where the meeting is held **any time before** the start of the meeting. IC 5-14-1.5-4(a). (This is not to be confused with the duty to post the notice of the occurrence of the meeting, which must be done at least forty-eight hours in advance, excluding weekend days and legal holidays.)

F. A governing body's action is **declared void**, if that action is the adoption of a rule, regulation, or other final action (e.g., the vote to cancel a teacher's contract) "**by reference to agenda number or item alone**. IC 5-14-1.5-4(a).

1. This provision is troublesome, especially in light of numerous school boards using "consent" items on their agendas.

2. The Indiana Public Access Counselor has rendered two school-related opinions where the first opined that the board's action was void, but in the second case with a different school board, the action was not void; the facts of the two situations were very similar and it is hard to grasp the conceptual difference. This indicates that courts would likely struggle as well if the issue were litigated. Therefore, when the action to be taken involves a significant matter like building construction or dismissal of a contracted employee, avoid litigation altogether by removing the issue from the consent portion of the agenda and proposing its adoption or approval by speaking to its subject matter and **not** to its agenda number or agenda item.

G. As the meeting progresses, memoranda are required to be kept regarding (1) the date, time, and place of the meeting, (2) the members of the governing body recorded as either present or absent, (3) the general substance of all matters proposed, discussed, or decided, and (4) a record of all votes taken, by individual members if there is a roll call. IC 5-14-1.5-4(b).

1. The memoranda are required to be available within a reasonable period of time after the meeting for the purpose of informing the public of the governing body's proceedings.

2. If the governing body uses minutes (all school boards apparently do), they must be open for public inspection and copying.

3. The memoranda requirement, as well as the minutes, if any, apply to **all meetings** of a school board, including executive sessions.

a. However, the executive session section, IC 5-14-1.5-6.1(d), allows modification pertaining to what was considered by stating that executive session minutes/memoranda "must identify the subject matter considered by specific reference to the enumerated instance or instances for which public notice was given." In other words, if the public notice stated the reason for the session was to discuss strategy with regard to collective bargaining, the minutes/memoranda (in addition to the other particulars like who was present and date, time, and place) only need state that the board discussed collective bargaining strategy.

b. Secondly, for executive session section of the ODL also states, "The governing body shall certify by a statement in the memoranda and minutes of the governing body that no subject matter was discussed in the executive session other than the subject matter specified in the public notice." *Id.*

H. Public notice of **all school board meetings** (regular and special, which includes executive sessions), **except for meetings where notice by publication is required by statute, e.g., a budget hearing)** is required. This requirement causes much difficulty to veteran and novice administrators and board members, alike. Error in administering the public notice section of the ODL results in any number of reactions, including critical newspaper articles, cancelled meetings, harm to efficient management of the system, threats of suit, litigation, Public Access Counselor Opinions on the state website revealing non-compliance by the offending board, board member, or administrator, and attacks on school board member incumbents from challengers at election time indicating ignorance or deliberate violation of the ODL. The public notice of meetings requirements at IC 5-14-1.5-6 establishes the following rules:

1. Public notice of the date, time, and place of **regular meetings** need only be given once each year (unless the date, time, or place of the meeting is changed). Executive sessions cannot be regular meetings under the ODL.

2. Public notice of the date, time, and place of all other meetings, including executive sessions, other special meetings, and statutory meetings must:

a. Be made at least forty-eight (48) hours before the meeting (not counting Saturdays, Sundays, and legal holidays).

(1) Emergency meetings are excepted from the forty-eight hour notice requirement.

(2) Reconvened meetings are also excepted **as long as** announcement of the date, time, and place of the reconvened meeting is made at the original meeting and recorded in the memoranda/minutes thereof, and the agenda is not changed. **However, executive session meetings may not be reconvened.**

3. Public notice **shall be given by:**

a. **posting a copy of the notice at the principal office** of the public agency holding the meeting or, if no such office exists, at the building where the meeting is to be held (at least 48 hours in advance, excluding Saturday, Sunday, and a legal holiday); **and**

b. **delivering notice to all news media which deliver by January 1 an annual written request for such notices for the next succeeding calendar year to the governing body** of the public agency (at least 48 hours in advance, excluding Saturday, Sunday, and a legal holiday).

c. **Delivery of the notice** shall be done by **one** of the following methods (48 hours in advance of the meeting, excluding Saturday, Sunday, and a legal holiday):

(1) **depositing the notice in the United States mail with postage prepaid;**

(2) **Transmitting the notice by electronic mail; or**

(3) **Transmitting the notice by facsimile (fax).**

4. **If a meeting is called to deal with an emergency** involving **actual or threatened injury to person or property**, or **actual or threatened disruption of the governmental activity** under the jurisdiction of the public agency by any event, then **the time requirements of notice under this section shall not apply, but:**

(a) news media which have requested notice of meetings must be given the **same notice as is given to the members of the governing body**; and

(b) the public must be notified by **posting a copy of the notice** at the principal office of the school system.

5. The above-stated requirements as to the 48-hour advance public notice by posting and delivery to news media are expressly stated **not to apply "where notice by publication is required by statute, ordinance, rule, or regulation."** IC 5-14-1.5-5(e). Therefore, the proper legal advertisement of a budget hearing, for example, makes it unnecessary to publicly post and deliver notice to news media in advance.

6. Error can still occur even if all of the above-requirements have been perfectly followed, and that is when the very last subsection (h) of IC 5-14-1.5-5 has not been followed. It states (bold added for emphasis):

Notice has **not** been given in accordance with this section **if a governing body** of a public agency **convenes a meeting at a time so unreasonably departing from the time stated** in its public notice that the **public is misled or substantially deprived of the opportunity to attend, observe, and record the meeting**.

I. Executive session meetings of school boards that can be held without any member of the public in attendance are controlled by IC 5-14-1.5-6.1.

1. The specific instances for holding executive sessions that apply to school boards are listed in subsection 6.1(b):

a. Where authorized by federal or state statute, such as the federal Family Educational Rights and Privacy Act that requires confidentiality of most education records of students.

b. For discussion of strategy with respect to (a) collective bargaining, (b) initiation of litigation or litigation that is either pending or has been threatened specifically in writing, (c) the implementation of security systems, and (d) the purchase or lease of real property by the governing body up to the time a contract or option to purchase or lease is executed by the parties (**provided, however**, that all of these strategy discussions must be necessary for competitive or bargaining reasons and **may not include competitive or bargaining adversaries**).

Thus, representatives of the teacher's union, could not be invited to a school board executive session under this strategy discussion provision.

c. For discussion of the assessment, design, and implementation of school safety and security measures, plans, and systems.

d. To receive information about and interview prospective employees.

e. With respect to any individual over whom the governing body has jurisdiction:

(1) to receive information concerning the individual's alleged misconduct; and

(2) to discuss, before a determination, the individual's status as an employee, a student, or an independent contractor who is either a physician or a school bus driver.

f. For discussion of records classified as confidential by state or federal statute.

g. To discuss before a placement decision an individual student's abilities, past performance, behavior, and needs.

h. To discuss a job performance evaluation of individual employees. This subdivision does not apply to a discussion of the salary, compensation, or benefits of employees during a budget process.

i. When considering the appointment of a public official, to do the following:

(1) Develop a list of prospective appointees.

(2) Consider applications.

(3) Make one initial exclusion of prospective appointees from further consideration.

(4) A school board may release and shall make available for inspection and copying in accordance with IC 5-14-3-3 (Access to Public Records Act) identifying information concerning prospective appointees not initially excluded from further consideration. An initial exclusion of prospective appointees from further consideration may not reduce the number of prospective appointees to fewer than three (3) unless there are fewer than three (3) prospective appointees. Interviews of prospective appointees must be conducted at a meeting that is open to the public.

j. To train school board members with an outside consultant about the performance of the role of the members as public officials.

k. To discuss information and intelligence intended to prevent, mitigate, or respond to the threat of terrorism.

2. Further rules regarding executive session meetings under IC 5-14-1.5-6.1 state:

a. A final action (i.e., a vote, by definition) must be taken at a meeting open to the public.

See the Indiana Court of Appeals decision in *Baker v. Town of Middlebury*, 753 N.E.2d 67 (Ind.App. 2001), which ruled that a governing body may reach a decision in executive session without violating the ODL, as long as no vote is taken at the closed session, and a public vote is made at a properly called open meeting.

b. **Public notice** of the executive session **is required to state the subject matter by specific reference to the enumerated instance or instances for which executive sessions may legally be held under IC 5-14-1.5-6.1(b).**

c. Memoranda/minutes of an executive session are required as in all meetings under IC 5-14-1.5-4, but are modified to require the identification of the subject matter considered by specific reference to the enumerated instance(s) for which the public notice was given.

d. The governing body **shall certify by a statement in the memoranda and minutes** of the governing body **that no subject matter was discussed in the executive session other than the subject matter specified in the public notice**.

e. A governing body **may not** conduct an executive session **during a meeting,** except as otherwise permitted by applicable statute. A meeting **may not be recessed and reconvened with the intent of circumventing this subsection**.

J. The ODL at IC 5-14-1.5-6.5 establishes the following rules regarding collective bargaining and discussion between the school board or any person it authorizes and the exclusive representative of teachers:

1. Any party may inform **the public** of the status of collective bargaining or discussion as it progresses by **release of factual information** and **expression of opinion based upon factual information**.

2. If a mediator is appointed, any report the mediator may file at the conclusion of mediation is a public record open to public inspection.

3. If a factfinder is appointed, any hearings the factfinder holds must be open at all times for the purpose of permitting members of the public to observe and record them.

4. Any findings and recommendations the factfinder makes are public records open to public inspection as provided by IC 20-29-8-13 (Collective Bargaining Law) or any other applicable statute relating to factfinding in connection with public collective bargaining.

K. The methods of enforcement of the ODL in a judicial proceeding, including suit, remedies, costs, and attorney fees are covered at IC 5-14-1.5-7.

L. All "public agencies" as defined by the ODL are prohibited from holding a meeting at a location that is not accessible to a person with a disability.

OVERTIME AND MINIUM WAGE REQUIREMENTS
UNDER THE FAIR LABOR STANDARDS ACT (FLSA)
29 USC section 201 *et seq*.; 29 Code of Federal Regulations Parts 510 to 794

Points of Emphasis:

A. For "nonexempt" school employees (basically those who are not administrators, teachers, or other qualifying "executive, administrative, or professional" employees as determined by the technical requirements of the FLSA), the Act requires the payment of minimum hourly wages and the payment of overtime for hours worked in excess of 40 in a work week.

1. Schools need to make sure that their "nonexempt" employees (even if "salaried" or, like lay coaches, who are paid in only one or two installments) receive at least minimum hourly pay, which is presently $7.25 an hour.

2. Employers are required to keep a record of actual hours worked on a daily basis; so, for non-hourly-non-exempt employees (like secretaries, teaching assistants, and lay coaches), schools need to regularly check time cards and divide hours worked into pay received to assure the result equals or exceeds the minimum hourly rate.

B. Overtime standards require the employer to pay at least time-and-a-half the employee's regular hourly rate for each hour actually worked over forty in a workweek.

1. A workweek can be any period of 168 consecutive hours (seven consecutive days times twenty-four hours) that the employer establishes, but normally it is the calendar week.

2. If the employer is aware that an employee is choosing on the employee's own initiative to start work before the standard time and/ or to continue work at the end of the day, the additional hours must be recorded and the employee compensated, including overtime for hours in addition to forty in a work week. (This is an easily and often violated area, and if the employer fails to record these self-initiated

extra work hours, but the employee does, the court is very likely to uphold the employee's documentation and award double damages plus attorney fees, a very costly result for the employer.)

3. For employees eligible for overtime pay who work more than one job at different hourly rates, the regulations provide for a formula to calculate a weighted hour rate to compute what is multiplied by time-and-a-half.

4. A **"volunteer" exception from having to pay overtime exists** for an employee, like a teacher's aide or secretary, who voluntarily chooses to provide service in an extracurricular activity that is **not related to the normal employment** and who **receives a "nominal fee"** for that unrelated activity.

a. According to a Department of Labor written interpretation, a fee or stipend that does not exceed twenty percent of the normal pay for that position in an area determined by the U.S. Department of Labor is deemed "nominal."

b. In an important federal circuit court of appeals case ruling over a school-related volunteer-nominal-stipend exception, the Fourth Circuit decided in the school's favor. The court found that the employee had not been coerced into taking the coaching position, which was not related to his security guard duties, and that his extracurricular stipend, when divided by the total hours spent, paid him less than the federal minimum wage. *Purdham v. Fairfax County Sch. Bd.*, 637 F.3d 421 (4th Cir. 2011).

5. The FLSA prohibits an employee from waiving any rights under the Act.

6. Governmental employers, including public schools, may choose to offer compensatory time at a rate of time-and-a-half for each hour worked over forty in a work week; the Act caps the total "comp time" that can be taken by any one employee to 240 hours.

C. The FLSA subjects employers to certain penalties which can include:

1. Criminal prosecution for willful violations of the Act with a maximum fine of $10,000. More than one willful violation can result in imprisonment.

2. Civil penalties may be assessed for employers who repeatedly violate the Act in an amount of up to $1000 for each violation.

D. Individual employees may enforce the Act by court action, and if successful, obtain "liquidated damages" in an amount that is double the wages owed.

1. If the employer has not kept track of the hours worked, courts will accept the employee's calculations into evidence if reasonable and made in good faith.

2. If the employee succeeds in the suit, the employer is required to pay the attorney's fees and expenses.

3. The period of time over which the double damages are calculated is normally two years.

E. A quality article entitled "Working Overtime" by Laura Smith, Assistant Editor, *Athletic Management*, 16 .5, August/September 2004, may be found at:

http://www.momentummedia.com/articles/am/am1605/overtime.htm.

It details the realities of the widespread litigation nationally against schools for overtime violations and the preventive reaction to avoid suit by the school board of Akron (Ohio) City Schools that, of unfortunate necessity, devastated the athletic department due to its large number of noncertified staff who also served as coaches at the end of the day..

F. Further excellent resources are provided by:

1. The North Carolina School Boards Association at: http://www.ncsba.org/flsa.htm; and

2. The federal Department of Labor at: http://www.dol.gov/index.htm.

PRAYER (See Chapter Twelve in the main text.)

Points of Emphasis:

A. Due to Free Exercise of Religion Clause of the First Amendment, students have the right to voluntarily pray during the school day on their own time, free time, or silently at any time so long as it does not create a substantial disruption to the school environment. They may not infringe on others students' rights or force others to listen.

B. Under the Equal Access Act (see EQUAL ACCESS ACT in this Article, above,) student-initiated groups at the high-school level, that meet at times when noncurriculum related groups are allowed to meet, are permitted to engage in prayer and other religious speech without discrimination (as long as the adult supervisor at religious meetings does not participate in the activity).

C. Public schools are prohibited by the Establishment of Religion Clause of the First Amendment, which compels neutrality toward religion, from promoting, sponsoring, or endorsing prayer.

PROCEDURAL DUE PROCESS FOR STUDENTS IC 20-33-8 (See Chapter Six in the main text and DISCIPLINE in this Article, above.)

PROCEDURAL DUE PROCESS FOR TEACHERS IC 20 28-7.5 (See Chapters Three and Four in the main text and TEACHER DISMISSAL in this Article, below.)

PUBLIC RECORDS ACCESS IC 5-14-3

Points of Emphasis:

A. The Indiana Access to Public Records Act (APRA) declares that it is the state's public policy "that all persons are entitled to full and complete information regarding the affairs of government and the official acts of those who represent them as public officials and employees," and that APRA "shall be liberally construed to implement this policy and place the burden of proof for the nondisclosure of a public record on the public agency that would deny access to the record and not on the person seeking to inspect and copy the record." IC 5-14-3-1.

B. "Public record" is defined to mean "any writing, paper, report, study, map, photograph, book, card, tape recording, or other material that is created, received, retained, maintained, or filed by or with a public agency and which is generated on paper, paper substitutes, photographic media, chemically based media, magnetic or machine readable media, electronically stored data, or any other material, regardless of form or characteristics." IC 5-14-3-2(n).

1. This definition literally states that a public record is "other material... created, received, retained, maintained, or filed by or with a public agency and which is generated on ... other material...."

2. The definition is so broad that the keys to the superintendent's office, as well to the safe inside, are "public records."

3. Therefore, the major question under APRA is whether the "public record," whether it be the office keys, or an employee's resignation, must be disclosed via inspection and/or copying to any person who so requests.

C. "Public agency" is defined broadly to include(1) a school corporation or any committee, instrumentality, or authority of the school corporation; (2) "other entity, or any office thereof, by whatever name designated, exercising in a limited geographical area the executive, administrative, judicial, or legislative power of the ... delegated local governmental power;" (3) any entity that the state board of accounts is required by law to audit; (4) any building corporation of a school corporation that issues bonds for construction of public facilities; and (5) any advisory committee created by statute to advise the school board. IC 5-14-3-2(m).

D. Any person may inspect and copy the public records of any public agency during the agency's regular business hours, **except for** public records listed in sections 4(a) (those required by state and federal law to be kept confidential) and 4(b) (those that the public agency may choose not to disclose). IC 5-14-3-3.

1. A request for inspection or copying must:

a. identify with **reasonable particularity** the record being requested; and

b. be made in writing on or in a form provided by the school corporation, if the school decides it must be in writing.

2. The school may not deny a request for disclosure because the requester does not state its purpose (unless another law requires the purpose to be stated).

3. If disclosure of a public record by copying is required (or in the school's discretion decided to be disclosed), the school must either (a) make the copies or (b) permit the requester to make copies on the school's equipment or the requester's own equipment.

4. Statutory rules for disclosure, nondisclosure, and methods of disclosure of maintained lists of names and addresses of employees and students are stated in IC 5-14-3-3(f).

a. Unless access to such lists are prohibited by law, the school is only required to permit the requester to inspect the lists and physically write down or manually type the information into the person's own computer.

b. Lists of names and addresses are prohibited from being disclosed in any manner to commercial and political entities for commercial and political purposes, respectively.

(1) This prohibition against disclosure applies to a list of school employees.

(2) The prohibition also applies to a list of enrolled students **but only if** the school board has adopted a policy. Indiana Code IC 5-14-3-3(f) (3) states:

(A) with respect to disclosure related to a commercial purpose, prohibiting the disclosure of the list to commercial entities for commercial purposes;

(B) with respect to disclosure related to a commercial purpose, specifying the classes or categories of commercial entities to which the list may not be disclosed or by which the list may not be used for commercial purposes; or

C) with respect to disclosure related to a political purpose, prohibiting the disclosure of the list to individuals and entities for political purposes.

A policy adopted under subdivision (3)(A) or (3)(B) must be uniform and may not discriminate among similarly situated commercial entities. For purposes of this subsection, "political purposes" means influencing the election of a candidate for federal, state, legislative, local, or school board office or the outcome of a public question or attempting to solicit a contribution to influence the election of a candidate for federal, state, legislative, local, or school board office or the outcome of a public question.

E. Records **required to be kept confidential** and that cannot be disclosed are listed at IC 5-14-3-4(a) as: (only listed are those applicable to schools)

1. Those declared confidential by state statute.

2. Those declared confidential by rule adopted by a public agency under specific authority to classify public records as confidential granted to the public agency by statute.

3. Those required to be kept confidential by federal law.

4. Confidential financial information obtained, upon request, from a person. However, this does not include information that is filed with or received by a public agency pursuant to state statute.

5. Grade transcripts and license examination scores obtained as part of a licensure process.

6. Those declared confidential by or under rules adopted by the supreme court of Indiana.

7. Patient medical records and charts created by a provider, unless the patient gives written consent under IC 16-39.

8. A Social Security number contained in the records of a public agency.

F. Records that **may be kept confidential** at the discretion of the school corporation are listed at IC 5-14-3-(b) as:

1. Investigatory records of law enforcement agencies. However, certain law enforcement records must be made available for inspection and copying as provided in section 5 of this chapter.

2. The work product of an attorney representing, pursuant to state employment or an appointment by a public agency: a public agency, the state, or an individual.

3. Test questions, scoring keys, and other examination data used in administering a licensing examination, examination for employment, or academic examination before the examination is given or if it is to be given again.

4. Scores of tests if the person is identified by name and has not consented to the release of the person's scores.

5. **Records that are intra-agency or interagency advisory or deliberative material,** including material developed by a private contractor under a contract with a public agency, **that are expressions of opinion or are of a speculative nature, and that are communicated for the purpose of decision making**.

6. **Diaries, journals, or other personal notes serving as the functional equivalent of a diary or journal**.

7. **Personnel files of public employees and files of applicants**

for public employment, *except for*: (All of the following **must** be disclosed.)

a. the name, compensation, job title, business address, business telephone number, job description, education and training background, previous work experience, or dates of first and last employment of present or former officers or employees of the agency;

b. information relating to the status of any formal charges against the employee; and

c. the factual basis for a disciplinary action in which final action has been taken and that resulted in the employee being suspended, demoted, or discharged.

However, all personnel file information shall be made available to the affected employee or the employee's representative. This subdivision does not apply to disclosure of personnel information generally on all employees or for groups of employees without the request being particularized by employee name.

(Also see TEACHER PERSONNEL RECORDS in this Article, below.)

8. Administrative or technical information that would jeopardize a record keeping or security system.

9. Computer programs, computer codes, computer filing systems, and other software that are owned by the public agency or entrusted to it and portions of electronic maps entrusted to a public agency by a utility.

10. Records specifically prepared for discussion or developed during discussion in an executive session under IC 5-14-1.5-6.1. However, this subdivision does not apply to that information required to be available for inspection and copying under subdivision (8).

11. The identity of a donor of a gift made to a public agency if: the donor requires nondisclosure of the donor's identity as a condition of making the gift, or after the gift is made, the donor or a member of the donor's family requests nondisclosure.

12. School safety and security measures, plans, and systems, including emergency preparedness plans developed under 511 IAC 6.1-2-2.5.

13. A record or a part of a record, the public disclosure of which would have a reasonable likelihood of threatening public safety by exposing a vulnerability to terrorist attack. A record described under this subdivision includes: (omitted)

G. If a requested public record contains some material that cannot be disclosed or that the school may choose not to disclose, at public expense the confidential material must be removed (redacted) so that the requester may view and receive a copy of the remaining portion. IC 5-14-3-6.

H. As a public agency, a school is required to protect public records from "loss, alteration, mutilation, or destruction," as well as to "regulate any material interference with the regular discharge of the duties of the public agency or public employees." IC 5-14-3-7.

1. This means that the school at its expense will very likely have to assign an employee to watch the requester go through its records.

2. It also means that the school will have a reasonable amount of time to go over the requested material and perform the copying work (which could be weeks under such circumstances as the volume of requested material, an employee missing due to illness, or other exigent situations).

I. A public agency is expressly prohibited from charging any fee for the cost of its employee's time for the inspection of the public record or "to search for, examine, or review a record to determine whether the record may be disclosed." IC 5-14-3-8.

a. A public agency is required to establish a uniform fee schedule for certifying and copying documents.

b. The agency may charge the either ten cents per page for non-color copies or the **actual cost** of copying if this can be shown to be more than ten cents per page (twenty-five cents if the page is in color).

"Actual cost" of copying is defined to exclude labor and overhead costs.

J. The rules governing a "denial of disclosure" are stated at IC 5-14-3-9, and cover the following situations:

1. When the requester is **physically present** in the public agency's office, or **makes the request by telephone**, or **requests "enhanced access"** to a document (i.e., by an electronic device other than that of the public agency's), a denial occurs if the requester **is refused** (by the agency's designated public record's official) *or* **twenty-four hours elapse and the requester is not given access by inspection or a copy**, *whichever occurs first*.

2. If the request is **for a copy** of the record and is made by **mail** or by **facsimile**, a denial of disclosure does not occur until **seven days have elapsed** from the date the public agency receives the request. (Presumably, the Legislature would have intended for an e-mail request to come within the seven-day rule. See the statute quoted in the next section indicating when a request is made by "enhanced access," i.e., a computer.)

3. The manner in which the agency may make the denial of disclosure is stated by IC 5-14-3-9(c) (bold added for emphasis):

(c) If a request is made orally, either in person or by telephone, a public agency may deny the request orally. However, if a request initially is made in writing, by facsimile, or through enhanced access, or if an oral request that has been denied is renewed in writing or by facsimile, a public agency **may deny the request if**:

(1) the denial is in writing or by facsimile; and

(2) the **denial includes:**

(A) **a statement of the specific exemption or exemptions authorizing the withholding of all or part of the public record;** and

(B) the **name and the title or position of the person responsible for the denial.**

4. It is not a denial of disclosure if the school official responsible for public records responds within the allotted time limit and informs the requester, for example, that it will take some time for the request to be evaluated, perhaps by legal counsel, and for the material to be reviewed in order to reach a decision on what, if any, material may be inspected or copied.

K. The statutory sections covering legal action, burden of proof, and attorney fees may be reviewed at IC 5-14-3-9, subsections (e) through (j).

PUBLIC RECORDS RETENTION AND DESTRUCTION
IC 5-15-6

Points of Emphasis:

A. The section of the Local Public Records Commission Statute that immediately catches a school administrator's attention is IC 5-15-6-8, which establishes a Class D felony for improper destruction or damage to a public record. It states (bold added for emphasis):

Sec. 8. A public official or other person who **recklessly, knowingly, or intentionally** destroys or damages any public record commits a **Class D felony unless:**

(1) the commission shall have given its **approval in writing that the public records may be destroyed;**

(2) the commission shall have entered its **approval for destruction of the public records on its own minutes;** or

(3) authority for destruction of the records is **granted by an approved retention schedule** established under this chapter.

1. The "commission" referred to is the county commission of public records for each of the state's 92 counties, whose members are stated in section 1 of IC 5-15-6 and includes the superintendent of schools of the school district in which the county seat is located.

The duties of the county commission are simply stated at IC 5-15-6-2 as the determination of:

(1) Which public records, if any, are no longer of official or historical value

(2) Which public records are of current official value and should be retained in the office where they are required to be filed

(3) Which public records are of official value but are consulted and used so infrequently that they are no longer of appreciable value to the officer with whom they are required to be filed

(4) Which public records are of no apparent official value but which do have historical value.

2. The term "public record" or "record" is defined in reference to the definition in the State Public Records Commission Statute at IC 5-15-5.1-1, except that state government means local government. The definition reads as follows with "[local]" inserted in place of the word "state." (Bold is added for emphasis.)

"Record" means all documentation of the informational, communicative or decisionmaking processes of [local] government, its agencies and subdivisions made or received by any agency of [local] government or its employees **in connection with the transaction of public business or government functions**, which documentation is created, received, retained, maintained, or filed by that agency or its successors as evidence of its activities or because of the informational value of the data in the documentation, and which is generated on:

(1) paper or paper substitutes;

(2) photographic or chemically based media;

(3) magnetic or machine readable media; or

4) any other materials, regardless of form or characteristics.

Because the term applies to those records that relate to the "transaction of public business or government functions," a personal document such as a school employee's personal calendar or an e-mail from a school employee's spouse to pick up milk and bread on the way home is not a record subject to retention.

3. The key provisions relating to school corporation retention of public records are found at IC 5-15-6-2.5 (bold added for emphasis):

Sec. 2.5. (a) The county commission shall **adopt and implement retention schedules** for use by local government officials as part of a records management program for local government public records at the first meeting of the county commission after the commission receives a retention schedule for the local government approved by the oversight committee on public records as established by IC 5-15-5.1-18.

(b) **All requests to destroy, transfer, or otherwise dispose of records that are not covered by an approved retention schedule are to be submitted to the county commission** according to the procedure established under this chapter.

(c) **Requests for exceptions to an approved retention schedule shall be submitted to the county commission.** The commission may not consider requests for retention of records that are shorter in duration than the approved retention schedule.

(d) **Local government officers shall submit documentation of destruction, transfer, or other disposal of records according to an approved retention schedule to the county commission** with a copy submitted to the state archives.

(e) Whenever a local government includes parts of more than one (1) county, the commission of the county that contains the greatest percentage of population of the local government has jurisdiction over the records of the local government for the purposes of this chapter.

a. Not all county public records commissions have adopted retention schedules.

b. Consequently, school districts in these counties will have to request and obtain written approval from the county commission before destroying any and all public records.

c. Schools in counties that have adopted a record retention schedule may destroy any public record listed thereon after the stated date for destruction, and then will have to complete and submit a state form of the records destroyed.

d. Any record that is not found on the county retention schedule **must be kept a minimum of three years** before submitting a request to destroy it. IC 5-15-6-3(b).

B. Due to recently revised rules of federal and state judicial procedure, schools need to be aware of and take measures to ensure that electronic records that may be subject to discovery in a lawsuit are preserved for the duration of the suit.

C. The following significant websites are very helpful in providing guidance to the school administrator in complying with the duty to preserve and properly destroy public records:

1. http://www.in.gov/icpr/ (Indiana Commission on Public Records)

2. http://www.in.gov/icpr/2272.htm   (County / Local Government Records Management)

3. http://www.in.gov/icpr/files/schoolretentionschedule.pdf (Indiana Public Schools General Retention Schedule) [Remember that this schedule **is a model only and may be used if** the county public records commission wherein the school district is located has actually adopted it.]

Q-S

RESIGNATIONS IC 5-8-3.5, IC 5-8-4

Points of Emphasis:

A. A public officer who is a school board member must give written notice of the resignation to the circuit court clerk of the county containing the largest percentage of population in the school corporation. IC 5-8-3.5-1.

B. A public school employee or school board member who submits a written resignation, whether to be effective immediately, when accepted, or at some future fixed date, with the proper person, persons, or authority of government to receive the resignation, the employee or board member has no right to withdraw, rescind, annul, or amend it without the consent of the person or entity having the power to fill the vacancy. IC 5-8-4-1.

1. Any condition in any resignation, except as to the time of taking effect, is "null and void." IC 5-8-4-2.

2. A school board member's written resignation is effective at the time of filing with the proper person (circuit court clerk), unless it contains a delayed effective date (or is permitted to be withdrawn, rescinded, annulled, or amended. IC 5-8-4-4.

3. The 2011 Indiana Teacher Contract Law states that a teacher's contract "continues in force ... for the next school term ... unless ... the teacher delivers **in person** or by **registered or certified mail** to the school corporation the teacher's **written** resignation." IC 20-28-7.5-7(a)(2).

C. Despite the above statutes regarding written resignations and the rules that apply thereto, **resignations may be oral** according to the Indiana Supreme Court in the case of *State ex rel. Palm v. City of Brazil*, 73 N.E.2d 485 (Ind. 1947), which upheld the oral statements of some tenured police officers and firemen made to the Mayor and members of the Board of Public Works and Safety that "they and each of them were walking off their respective jobs and quitting same on August 1st, 1945." *Id.* at 487.

D. A school board may accept, as a resignation, the teacher's or other employee's **abandonment of position** if the facts are sufficiently clear that the person's conduct demonstrated the intent to voluntarily relinquish the position.

1. The Supreme Court of Michigan in *Tomiak v. Hamtramck School District*, 397 N.W. 2d 770 (Mich. 1986), ruled that a teacher had abandoned his right to be recalled to a teaching position, and expressed its rationale for applying the "abandonment doctrine" at page 776 (bold added for emphasis):

> Because the Court of Appeals remanded for a hearing, the questions raised by the abandonment doctrine and its application here were not decided below. However, the circuit court and the Tenure Commission both accepted its use in this state, as well as its application to the facts here. We agree. As the circuit court ably reasoned:
>
>> "Clearly, the abandonment doctrine cannot be employed against a tenured teacher who manifests every intention of continuing on the job. But **it is equally clear that a local board must have some legal mechanism with which to treat those employees who for whatever reason, refuse to work and refuse to verbalize a resignation.** The abandonment doctrine provides that tool. It has been accepted and affirmed in several Michigan cases *Johnson v Taylor School District, ... Purcell v Ferndale School District, ... Carswell v Wayne-Westland Schools...* It is an established legal principle in Michigan."

2. The Indiana Court of Appeals has impliedly accepted the resignation by abandonment doctrine, but due to the specific facts of the case did not find that it had occurred in *Board of School Trustees of Salem Community Schools v. Robertson*, 637 N.E.2d 181, (Ind.App. 1994). Said the court at page 186:

> The Board argues that Robertson "voluntarily abandoned her position and/or waived any further rights by failing to report to work in the fall of 1988 and expressly giving 'authorization' to hire a 'permanent replacement.' ... [W]hether characterized as a mutual rescission, voluntary quit, abandonment, or waiver, [Robertson] should be precluded from claiming additional entitlements."... We disagree.

> In order for a teacher's conduct to be interpreted by a school
> board as a resignation, it must be shown that the resignation
> was voluntary and intentional. *Joyce v. Hanover Community
> Sch. Corp.* (1971) ... 276 N.E.2d 549, 555, *overruled in part
> on other* grounds... Similarly, a waiver is "a voluntary yielding
> up of some existing right, ... an intentional relinquishment
> of a known right involving both knowledge of the existence
> of the right and the intention to relinquish it." *Shelt v. Baker*
> (1922)...137 N.E. 74 ... (1923).

Contrary to the Board's position, the material facts reveal only
that Robertson wanted to take the full one-year maternity leave
to which she was entitled *and* to retain her teaching position.
The facts simply do not support the conclusion that Robertson
voluntarily quit or abandoned her position.

E. The argument that the resignation was made under duress or
coercion will be rejected as long as the **employer gives the employee
an option of dismissal or resignation**. See *Board of School Com'rs
of City of Indianapolis v. State ex rel. Bever*, 5 N.E.2d 307 (Ind. 1936)
where the Supreme Court stated at page 309:

> The contention that her resignation was not voluntary finds no
> support unless it be in the fact that the communication from the
> school authorities amounted to a threat to remove her and cancel
> her contract because of the quality of her work. But a notice that
> a contract will be canceled for good and legal cause cannot be
> construed as a threat and made the basis of a charge of coercion
> or duress. The school authorities had a legal right to determine
> whether her services were satisfactory, and, if they were not,
> the right to prefer charges, and to remove her if the evidence
> warranted. They had the undoubted right to apprise her of their
> intention in advance, and to tender her the opportunity of canceling
> her contract and resigning. This they did. Their action is as readily
> attributable to courtesy and consideration for her feelings as to an
> improper motive.

In the *Bever* case, the acting school superintendent had written the
permanent teacher stating:

The quality of your work has been such that there is no place in which we can use you. If you care to have your record show that you resigned, your resignation will be accepted.

Bever responded by saying, "I would prefer that my name appear under resignations rather than under a list as being dropped if it is necessary." This was treated and accepted by the school board as a resignation, and the Supreme Court agreed by stating at pages 308-309 (bold added for emphasis):

> Rights of parties under their contracts must be determined upon the theory that they knew and correctly interpreted the law affecting their interests. If they compromise, cancel, **or abandon their contracts** under a misapprehension as to the rights or remedies which the law may afford them, the law will not reinstate the contracts upon discovery of their misapprehension and proof of their mistake... It may be that she preferred resignation to a hearing upon her record, but whatever her motive, she had the right to choose, and **the communication can only be interpreted as a choice of resignation rather than termination** of her tenure by action of the school authorities....

SEARCH AND SEIZURE IC 20-33-8-32
(See Chapters Three and Seven in the main text.)

Points of Emphasis:

A. The Fourth Amendment to the United States Constitution and cases interpreting it set the legal standards for public school searches and seizures involving students and employees.

B. The landmark student search case is *New Jersey v. T.L.O.*, 469 U.S. 325 (1985), where the Supreme Court established the legal standard applicable to students at pages 341-342 (bold added for emphasis):

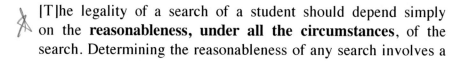

> [T]he legality of a search of a student should depend simply on the **reasonableness, under all the circumstances,** of the search. Determining the reasonableness of any search involves a

[handwritten margin note: What we use to determine all other cases]

twofold inquiry: first, one must consider "**whether the ... action was justified at its inception**," ... second, one must determine **whether the search as actually conducted "was reasonably related in scope to the circumstances which justified the interference in the first place**," ... Under ordinary circumstances, **a search of a student by a teacher or other school official will be "justified at its inception" when there are reasonable grounds for suspecting that the search will turn up evidence that the student has violated or is violating either the law or the rules of the school.** Such a search will be **permissible in its scope when the measures adopted are reasonably related to the objectives of the search and not excessively intrusive in light of the age and sex of the student and the nature of the infraction.**

(Note that the Supreme Court established the *T.L.O.* "reasonable scope-reasonable suspicion" standard for individual school employee searches and seizures in the case of *O'Connor v. Ortega*, 480 U.S. 709 (1987).)

C. The Supreme Court later modified the *T.L.O.* individual student search standard in the following two cases involving drug testing of multiple students in athletics and other extracurricular activities on a random basis without the need for individualized reasonable suspicion:

1. *Vernonia School Dist. 14J v. Acton*, 515 U.S. 646 (1995), upheld as "reasonable under all the circumstances" the "suspicionless" drug testing of athletes whose names were selected on a random basis. The Court's rationale, in part, was expressed at pages 652-653:

As the text of the Fourth Amendment indicates, **the ultimate measure of the constitutionality of a governmental search is "reasonableness."** At least in a case such as this, . . . whether a particular search meets the reasonableness standard "**is judged by balancing its intrusion on the individual's Fourth Amendment interests against its promotion of legitimate governmental interests.**"...

2. *Board of Education of Indep. Sch. Dist. No. 92 v. Earls*, 536 U.S. 822 (2002), upheld a suspicionless, random drug testing policy that

applied not only to athletics, but all extracurricular activities, and stated its rationale at pages 836-838 (bold added for emphasis):

> The drug abuse problem among our Nation's youth has hardly abated since *Vernonia* was decided in 1995. In fact, evidence suggests that it has only grown worse. As in *Vernonia*, "the necessity for the State to act is magnified by the fact that this evil is being visited not just upon individuals at large, but upon children for whom it has undertaken a special responsibility of care and direction." . . . The health and safety risks identified in *Vernonia* apply with equal force to Tecumseh's children. Indeed, **the nationwide drug epidemic makes the war against drugs a pressing concern in every school**...

> Likewise, the **need to prevent and deter the substantial harm of childhood drug use provides the necessary immediacy** for a school testing policy. Indeed, it would make little sense to require a school district to wait for a substantial portion of its students to begin using drugs before it was allowed to institute a drug testing program designed to deter drug use...

> Respondents also argue that the **testing of nonathletes** does not implicate any safety concerns, and that safety is a "crucial factor" in applying the special needs framework. . . . They contend that there must be "surpassing safety interests," . . . or "extraordinary safety and national security hazards," . . . in order to override the usual protections of the Fourth Amendment. . . . Respondents are correct that safety factors into the special needs analysis, but **the safety interest furthered by drug testing is undoubtedly substantial for all children, athletes and nonathletes alike.** We know all too well that drug use carries a variety of health risks for children, including death from overdose....

3. Indiana's Locker Search Statute, IC 20-33-8-32, requires school boards to adopt a locker search policy and give notice of such to students and parents. (The most effective way is to publish the policy in the student discipline handbook.)

a. Although the statute declares that the lockers are the property of the school, that students have no expectation of privacy in the lockers or their contents, and that principals may search the lockers and their contents at any time subject to school board policy, school officials **must remember that there is a constitutional expectation of privacy in such student-owned possessions as jackets, book bags, and cell phone messages and pictures** that may be kept in a locker.

b. Therefore, reasonable suspicion to believe that a personal item within a locker contains evidence of a rule violation before a search is commenced.

T ▬▬▬▬▬▬▬▬

TEACHER DISMISSAL IC 20-28-7.5
(See Chapter Four in the main text.)

Points of Emphasis:

A. The primary framework for the dismissal of teachers is the Indiana Teacher Contract Law, codified at IC 20-28-7.5.

1. The 2011 Indiana Legislature (1) repealed the 84 year old "tenure" law along with its "nonpermanent," "semipermanent," and "permanent teacher" designations; (2) replaced it with new teacher categories (**Probationary, Established, and Professional,** or **"PEP,"**); and (3) created a totally different dismissal process.

a. A **"probationary teacher"** is defined in such a way at IC 20-28-6-7.5(b) to mean a teacher first employed by a school corporation after June 30, 2011. In other words, it is a teacher first contracted for the 2011-2012 school year. This "2011-2012" teacher will remain "probationary" for said school year only, and if the contract continues for the 2012-2013 year, said teacher will become an "established" teacher and remain such for that teacher's entire career at that one school corporation.

b. An **"established teacher"** is one who served under contract as a teacher before July 1, 2012 and who entered into another teacher's contract by July 1, 2012. This category will include the huge majority of present teachers ranging from those who have taught in one corporation for 40+ years up to those who first began in 2011-2012 and continued into the next year. See IC 20-28-6-8. Established teachers will forever remain in this group as long as they continue employment with the corporation where they first became established.

c. A **"professional teacher"** is defined as one receiving a rating of effective or highly effective, or a combination of both under the 2011 Staff Performance Evaluation Plan Law for "at least three (3) years in a five (5) year or shorter period...." IC 20-28-6-7.5(c). Therefore, the first time that a teacher may "legally" be deemed "professional" will be at the conclusion of the 2013-2014 school year (by having received the requisite ratings starting in the 2011-2012 year, followed by the same in 2012-2013 and 2013-2014).

2. The federal Constitution's Fourteenth Amendment Due Process Clause must also be considered in certain dismissal situations where the sufficiency of due process is questioned and the school has to decide if additional procedures should be afforded (e.g., the teacher requests that school board members be questioned about their ability to fairly judge the matter.)

3. It is noted that due to 2011 changes in the Collective Bargaining Law, about one third of the 310 statewide bargaining units who bargained in 2011 no longer have master contract language regarding teacher dismissal procedures and binding arbitration of dismissals. As the other contracts expire, eventually none will contain teacher dismissal language due to statutory prohibitions in the Bargaining Law. Until the time comes when no contracts contain dismissal language, administrators will need to check their contracts to make sure there are no dismissal requirements to follow in addition to or in lieu of the statutory process.

B. The definition of "teacher" was changed in 2011 for purposes of teacher contracting and dismissal per IC 20-28 by establishing the requirement that a teacher, in addition to meeting the state licensure requirements, must be one "whose primary responsibility is the

instruction of students." See IC 20-18-2-22 which expressly *includes* the positions of superintendent, principal, and librarian within the definition. Therefore, unless an assistant superintendent or assistant principal has the primary duty of student instruction (as would, for example, an assistant superintendent of instruction), these former "teacher" positions, along with coordinators, directors, guidance counselors, social workers, deans, and varsity coaches and athletic directors, who do not sufficiently instruct students during the day, are not "teachers" within the definition.

1. For new persons employed into positions that require a license from IDOE, but who are not "teachers" under the 2011 definition because their primary function is not instruction, a school is not required to place them on a "Regular Teacher's Contract" and not required to follow the contract dismissal procedures in IC 20-28-7.5. It is submitted that schools may do so at their discretion.

2. Because of constitutional due process entitlement to those whom government employers had given a reasonable expectation of continued employment, which would be those persons who were previously considered "teachers" and who obtained continuing contract status ("tenure"), it is advisable to maintain those who are no longer "teachers" under the 2011 definition on the Regular Contract and provide them the statutory dismissal process under IC 20-28-7.5 as long as they continue to be employed in the previous position. However, in the situation where a long time counselor under a Regular Teacher's Contract became the athletic director, who does not instruct students, the school would have the right to determine that this new position is non-teaching, and the former counselor would no longer have the right to the continuing Regular Contract.

C. **Decline to Continue at End of Contract Process.** Certain teachers whom the principal has notified of his/her "preliminary decision" to "decline to continue" their contracts **may or may not have** the right to go through a conference process prior to the school board vote against continuation, but due to the confusing language of the dismissal statute, IC 20-28-7.5, it is advisable to offer a conference with the superintendent before the recommendation is made to the board to decline to continue it. This assumed process would only offer a conference with the superintendent without affording a second conference with the school board.

1. One group of teachers affected by this concept of the principal's "preliminary decision to decline to continue the contract are **probationary teachers** who (1) received an ineffective designation on the performance evaluation, (2) received two consecutive improvement necessary ratings on the evaluation, (3) are subject to a justifiable decrease in teaching positions (RIF), or (4) are subject to facts indicating that that the school has any reason relevant to its interests. IC 20-28-7.5-1(b).

a. A second type of **"probationary teacher"** under IC 20-28-6-7.5(b) is a teacher first contracted by a school corporation for the 2012-2013 school year (as well as all years thereafter). (It is also the 2012-2013 year when the new Staff Performance Evaluation Plan Law, IC 20-28-11.5, is to be implemented.) All probationary teachers from 2012-2013 on will remain such until becoming a **"professional teacher,"** which is defined as one receiving a rating of effective or highly effective, or a combination of both under the 2011 Staff Performance Evaluation Plan Law for "at least three (3) years in a five (5) year or shorter period...." IC 20-28-6-7.5(c).

b. A third type of **"probationary teacher"** occurs when a professional teacher is reduced in status. The statute at IC 20-28-6-7.5(d) reads:

> A professional teacher who receives a rating of ineffective in an evaluation under IC 20-28-11.5 shall be considered a probationary teacher but is not subject to the cancellation of the teacher's contract unless at least one (1) of the following criteria applies:
>
> (1) The teacher receives a rating of ineffective in an evaluation under IC 20-28-11.5 in the year immediately following the teacher's initial rating of ineffective.
> (2) The teacher's contract cancellation is due to a justifiable decrease in the number of teaching positions under IC 20-28-7.5-1(b)(3).
> (3) The teacher's contract cancellation is due to conduct set forth

in IC 20-28-7.5-1(b).

2. A second group of teachers whom the principal may notify of a "preliminary decision" to "decline to continue" their contracts are **established and professional teachers who are subject to a justifiable decrease in the number of positions (RIF).** IC 20-28-7.5-1(c). This means, for example, that a veteran, highly effective teacher can be dismissed at the end of a school year due to RIF via the relatively simple process of the school declining to continue the contract.

3. The only expressed process by the Legislature for **declining to continue a contract** appears at IC 20-28-7.5-2(a) where there is no mention of a conference, just the principal's notice of the preliminary decision to decline to continue the contract. For purposes of preventive law until the Legislature clarifies, or a court orders, a conference, it is advisable to offer a superintendent-level conference, which is the first step in the process to immediately cancel a contract. (The very next statutory subsection following the one dealing with declining to continue, IC 20-28-7.5-2(b), jumps to the totally different concept of a **cancellation of contract**, which is stated to be an **immediate** cancellation at IC 20-28-7.5-1(e), and contains the two-conference process discussed below.)

D. **Immediate Cancellation of Contracts Effective upon School Board's Vote.** If **any** category of teacher (i.e., probationary, established, or professional) is to be dismissed effective **before** the end of the school year or expiration of the contract's term, the controlling law is: (1) the Teacher Contract Law at IC 20-28-7.5, and (2) the Due Process Clause of the Fourteenth Amendment.

1. The process for immediate cancellation of contract begins with the principal's preliminary decision to cancel notice that must give the statutory reason(s) for the cancellation (that are listed at IC 20-28-7.5-1(e)), as well as notice that the teacher has five (5) days to request a private conference with the superintendent.

2. No details are given for the superintendent-level conference other

than the teacher is entitled to have a representative present and that after the conference the superintendent must make a written recommendation to the school board. If the teacher failed to request the conference, the principal's preliminary decision to cancel the contract is considered final, and per IC 20-26-5-4.5 the principal's decision goes to the school board for ultimate approval.

3. If the teacher within five (5) days following the first conference with the superintendent exercises the right to request a private conference with the school board, the type of conference will depend upon the reason(s) given for the contract cancellation.

a. A basic conference, no details of which are given in the statute, will be held when the reason relates to justifiable decrease in positions, incompetence, or a conviction for certain felonies. (This has been dubbed the "346" conference because the subsections of given reasons are 3, 4, and 6 of IC 20-28-7.5-1(e).)

b. A more elaborate conference must be given when the reason for cancellation relates to immorality, insubordination, neglect of duty, or other good or just cause. (This is the so-called "1257" conference.)

(1) Specified details of the 1257 conference allow the teacher to present evidence to refute the school's given reason(s), but both parties are expressly required to have exchanged such evidence at least seven (7) days in advance of the conference.

(2) At the 1257 conference, the school board is required to "consider whether a preponderance of the evidence supports the cancellation of the teacher's contract."

E. Additional provisions of the 2011 Teacher Contract Law, IC 20-28-7.5, include:

1. Pending the school board's final decision on a teacher's contract cancellation, the school is permitted to suspend the teacher from duty. However, the statute does **not** say whether the suspension is **with or without** pay. (Before the 2011 revision, it required the teacher to receive pay.) This leaves it up to each school and its legal counsel to

make the decision based on the particular facts and the strength of the governmental interests involved when compared to the teacher's interest. The classic U.S. Supreme Court's *Mathews v. Eldridge* constitutional balancing of interests test must be applied. (See Chapter Four of the main text.) There is Seventh Circuit case law supporting a suspension without pay followed by post-deprivation process within a reasonable timeframe. This could occur where the school board during its conference with the teacher, or a designated agent (e.g., the superintendent during the conference process), would consider both sides of the suspension without pay issue and make a determination as to whether to pay the amount in question. Because the time period is relatively short between the initial notice and the final school board conference, a reasonable argument exists that a school could suspend without pay at the time of the first notice of rights and then along with the consideration of the dismissal question determine if the teacher should or should not receive pay during the time leading up to the dismissal decision.

2. Absent a teacher's written resignation, the receipt of a new contract, or the school's refusal to continue (or cancellation of) a teacher's contract, it "continues on the same terms and for the same wages, unless increased under IC 20-28-9-1 for the next school term following the date of the contract's termination...." IC 20-28-7.5-6.

a. IC 20-28-9-1 is the salary increase statute (formerly called the minimum salary law) that ties wage increases to a four-part statutory formula weighted heavily on performance via a staff performance evaluation system under IC 20-28-11.5, which is to be implemented in the 2012-2013 school year. Under the new salary increase statute, only teachers rated as highly effective and effective will be entitled to raises.

b. This school-year-to-school-year-contract-continuation language replaces the 84-year-old "indefinite contract" status concept. It is noted, however, that only the classification of "established" teachers (those serving under contract as a teacher before July 1, 2012 and who entered into another teacher's contract by July 1, 2012) will have a "contract considered to continue indefinitely as an indefinite contract, subject to IC 20-28-7.5." IC 20-28-6-8. (This concept was for the likely purpose of maintaining the indefinite contract status of those teachers who had earned it, even though the statutory basis was repealed, due to the constitutional doctrine that prohibits a formerly legal contract from being impaired by legislative or executive decision.)

3. A school board and the exclusive representative of the teachers are expressly prohibited from "agreeing to binding arbitration of teacher dismissals." IC 20-28-7.5-7. (It is noted, however, that due to the impairment of contract doctrine, discussed in Chapter One of the main text, any present contract negotiated before July 1, 2011 that contains such binding arbitration will be valid until the contract's expiration date, or the date that both parties should mutually agree to reopen it.)

4. A contract signed by a teacher with a second school corporation after August 15, while still under contract with the first corporation, is void. The only way for the contract with the second school to be effective (valid) is when the teacher either (1) furnishes a release by the previous school or (2) "shows proof that thirty (30) days written notice was delivered by the teacher to the first employer." IC 20-28-7.5-8(b).

F. In order for a person to have the statutory, constitutional, and collective bargaining rights of a teacher, the person must be a "teacher" under the requirements of the teacher licensing code. See the discussion under the LICENSURE section, above, especially pertaining to Indiana case law holding that there can be no breach of contract by a school corporation for summarily dismissing a person from a teaching position who is not licensed, since a Teacher Contract with a non-licensed individual is void.

G. The following requirements and concepts contained in the Teacher Contract Law and case law interpreting it must be considered:

1. A Teacher Contract cannot be canceled for political or personal reasons.

2. The Indiana Court of Appeals in the case of *Fiscus v. Board of School Trustees of Central School Dist. of Greene County*, 509 N.E.2d

1137 (Ind.App. 1987), defined the contract cancellation ground of "immorality" at page 1141as:

> "not essentially confined to a deviation from sex morality; it may be such a course of conduct as offends the morals of the community and is a bad example to the youth whose ideals a teacher is supposed to foster and to elevate."

Note that courts, like Indiana's, require evidence of two things to meet the standard of proof of "immorality." The first is conduct below community standards, and the second, a negative impact on the teacher's fitness or ability to positively perform in the classroom, e.g., the conduct is a "bad example" (or negative role model) for children or hostile to the school community.

3. The cancellation ground of "insubordination" is defined in the statute as a "willful refusal to obey the state school laws or reasonable rules adopted for the governance of the school building or the school corporation." IC 20-28-7.5-1(e)(2).

a. The Indiana Court of Appeals provided further interpretation of "insubordination" in the case of *Werblo v. Hamilton Heights Sch. Corp.*, 519 N.E.2d 185 (Ind.App. 1988), where the court ruled against the school board because the principal's directive to Werblo was neither clear nor reasonable. As to not being clear, the principal issued one directive, followed later by a second that contradicted the first; and as to not being reasonable, the directive to attend a religiously-based convocation was illegal due to violating the Establishment of Religion Clause of the First Amendment.

b. A teacher's not following a reasonable and clear directive of a superior in order to be "willful" cannot be an action of neglect; for example, a reasonable and clear directive given orally by a principal at a teachers' meeting on the first day of school, and without any reinforcement with reminders throughout the year, is not likely to be remembered late in the school year. In such circumstance if contract cancellation is in order, the proper cause would be neglect of duty, not insubordination.

4. The contract cancellation ground of "other good or just cause" has been broadly interpreted by the Indiana Supreme Court in the case of *Board of School Trustees of School City of Peru v. Moore*, 33 N.E.2d 114 (Ind. 1941), where the court stated at page 116:

> 'Other good and just cause,' as used in this statute, has been held to mean any ground which is put forward in good faith, and which is not arbitrary, irrational, unreasonable, or irrelevant to the school board's task of building up and maintaining an efficient school system.

5. A licensed teacher employed on a Regular Teacher Contract who serves in an administrative position, but not one having its own nonrenewal of contract requirements like the positions of superintendent, assistant superintendent, principal, and assistant principal, does not have any right of process when removed from the administrative position and reassigned as a classroom teacher at lower pay; such action by the school is not a cancellation of contract under the Teacher Contract Law. See *Morton-Finney v. Gilbert*, 646 N.E.2d 1387 (Ind.App. 1995).

Note that the same principle of there being no need for the cancellation of contract process would most likely apply to a teacher in a non-administrative position, such as a counselor on an extended contract, who is reassigned to a teaching position at a lower pay, or merely reduced in days in the same position.

6. A teacher whose contract is being cancelled has no right to the discovery procedures of the trial rules; hence, no depositions or interrogatories can be utilized. See *Board of School Commissioners of Indianapolis Public Schools v. Walpole*, 801 N.E.2d 622 (Ind. 2004).

7. Judicial review of a school board's cancellation of a teacher's contract is conducted by a county court having jurisdiction over the school corporation. No traditional trial is held and no witnesses come before the judge and jury to have their testimony weighed and judged. Instead, oral and written arguments are presented to the judge who is not allowed to reweigh the evidence (i.e., give more or less importance to

the evidence presented to the school board). Under the judicial review doctrine stated in the case of *Harrison-Washington Comm. Sch. Corp. v. Bales*, 450 N.E.2d 559 (Ind.App. 1983), a school board's decision (which, based on case law, has to be reflected in written findings and conclusions adopted at an open meeting) to cancel a teacher's contract must be upheld if all of the following exist:

a. the school board followed proper Teacher Contract Law procedures, including the assignment of legal cause for contract cancellation;

b. there was substantial evidence to support the board's findings of legal cause; and

c. the hearing was fair.

In order to reverse a school board's contract cancellation under the judicial review doctrine, the legal burden is on the teacher to prove that the school board failed to comply with any one of the three stated criteria. See *Fiscus v. Board of School Trustees of Central School Dist. of Greene County*, 509 N.E.2d 1137 (Ind.App. 1987), where the Court of Appeals upheld the cancellation of a permanent teacher's contract and found that the testimony of five fifth-grade students who stated at the school board hearing that they heard their teacher use the obscenity "f---" during class constituted substantial evidence.

Although the 2011 Legislature stated that a school board must consider if a preponderance of the evidence supports contract cancellation, case law research indicates that upon judicial review, the court will apply the substantial evidence standard.

8. Under case law interpretation of the former "tenure law" contract cancellation ground of "justifiable decrease in the number of teaching positions," a teacher in the higher tenure category had to be retained over a teacher in a lower category when both are equally licensed to perform the position. See *Watson v. Burnett*, 23 N.E.2d 420 (Ind. 1939). This result has been reversed by the 2011 Legislature, which stated at IC 20-28-7.5-1(d):

After June 30, 2012, the cancellation of teacher's (*sic*) contracts due to justifiable decrease in the number of teaching positions shall be determined on the basis of performance rather than seniority. In cases where teachers are placed in the same performance category, any of the items in IC 20-28-9-1(b) may be considered.

Note, however, that some bargaining agreements with "RIF" language calling for seniority remain valid due to the constitutional impairment of contract doctrine discussed in Chapter One of the main text. Therefore, seniority clauses to determine "RIF" will be legal until the contract expires (or is reopened by the mutual consent of the school board and exclusive representative).

H. A comprehensive resource is the *2011 Employee Dismissal Manual* published by the Indiana School Boards Association.

TEACHER PERSONNEL FILE RECORDS IC 5-14-3-4(b)(8)
(Also see PUBLIC RECORDS ACCESS in this Article, above)

Points of Emphasis:

A. "All personnel file information shall be made available to the affected employee or the employee's representative."

B. The Indiana Access to Public Records Act (APRA) makes disclosure of employee personnel file information a discretionary decision of a public school corporation, except for the following:.

1. Under IC 5-14-3-4(a), a school is **prohibited from disclosing** such employee personnel file records as:

a. Records required to be kept confidential by state and federal law;

b. Grade transcripts and license examination scores;

c. Patient medical records created by a provider unless written consent is given; and

d. A Social Security number contained in the records of a public agency.

2. Under IC 5-14-3-4(b)(8), a school **is required to disclose** from an employee's personnel file:

> "(A) the name, compensation, job title, business address, business telephone number, job description, education and training background, previous work experience, or dates of first and last employment of present or former officers or employees of the agency;
>
> (B) information relating to the **status of any formal charges** against the employee; and
>
> (C) the **factual basis** for a disciplinary action in which **final action has been taken** and that resulted in the employee being **suspended, demoted, or discharged**."

a. "Final action" is not defined in APRA, and in the opinion of the Indiana Public Access Counselor, it means the final step that was taken in the suspension, demotion, or discharge; this could result in the particular disciplinary matter not going before the school board for a vote. (For example, if an employee administratively accepts a suspension without pay and waives the right to the statutory due process, the final action would be at the central office level.)

b. "Factual basis" in the opinion of the Public Access Counselor means the information contained in a document or record in the employee's personnel file (and not a written summary of that record prepared by an administrator or school attorney).

(1) If a court is asked to determined this issue, it will have to decide whether, for example, a tape recording in its entirety giving sensitive details of sexual harassment against a supervisor has to be disclosed, or whether it is valid for the school to merely state the reason for the suspension, demotion, or discharge as "an allegation of sexual harassment."

(2) A resignation from employment in the face of facts that could

reasonably be construed as sexual harassment would most likely be determined by a court as not a "discharge."

(3) An **administrative** suspension of an employee for the purpose of conducting an efficient investigation of a matter that could lead to suspension, demotion, or discharge would likely be found by a court not to be an act of discipline, and, thus, the "factual basis" for such a non-disciplinary suspension would not have to be disclosed.

(4) "Status of a formal charge" indicates where in the process the matter presently lies, e.g., investigation stage, proceeding toward suspension or dismissal stage, or conclusion stage wherein the school found insufficient facts to take action, issued an oral or written warning, or gave a written reprimand placing the employee on probation.

(5) "Formal charge" is not statutorily defined, so a school attorney, as would a court, would go to the dictionary for the commonly understood meaning of "formal."

TEACHER SUSPENSION IC 20-28-7.5-4; IC 20-28-9, sections 21-23

Points of Emphasis:

A. Suspension Pending Cancellation of Contract

The 2011 legislation removed the statutory requirement that a suspension pending contract cancellation procedure had to be with pay, and replaced it with language that merely states that a teacher may be suspended pending a final decision. IC 20-28-7.5-4.

1. This means that constitutional due process will be the controlling law where the teacher's interests in continued salary payments are balanced against the public school's interests in efficiency and protecting its budget. The U.S. Supreme Court in the case of *Gilbert v. Homar*, 520 U.S. 924 (1997), and the Seventh Circuit in two cases, *Ibarra v. Martin*, 143 F.3d 286 (7th Cir. 1998 and *Chaney v. Suburban*

Bus Division of the Regional Transportation Authority, 52 F.3d 623 (7th Cir. 1995), have upheld pre-due process suspensions without pay in situations where the government's interests are proven to outweigh those of the employee and the employee receives post-suspension due process within a reasonable period of time.

2. If the suspension pending cancellation is with pay, the Indiana Board of Accounts is of the audit position that this administrative decision must be ratified by the school board in order to prevent the issue of ghost employment from arising.

B. Disciplinary Suspensions Independent of Contract Cancellation

1. IC 20-28-9, sections 21-23, provide the required process when it is decided to suspend the teacher without pay as the only means of discipline. There is a minimum 30-day notice process before the school board can act, and a hearing is required if requested.

2. In the great majority of these situations, superintendents have been able to secure a written waiver of statutory and constitutional due process rights wherein the teacher agrees to accept the disciplinary suspension without pay.

TENURE IC 20-28, chapters 6 and 7.5 (See Chapter Four in the main text and TEACHER DISMISSAL in this Article, above.)

Points of Emphasis:

A. The term "tenure" is rarely used by the Indiana Legislature in a technical legal sense, but is utilized by courts and attorneys to refer to the condition where a teacher's contract is deemed to continue unless certain events occur, such as resignation or dismissal where the governmental employer is required to use certain processes (statutory and constitutional) to terminate the teacher's contract and right of continuation.

B. The 2011 Legislature repealed the former so-called "tenure" law, which had created an *indefinite contract* status for certain teachers whose contracts were considered to have continued indefinitely as long as the teachers displayed competence or were not "riffed."

1. The 2011 replacement statute, IC 20-28-7.5, simply created a continuing one-school- year to the next-school-year concept whereby a probationary teacher's contract could be declined continuation at the end of the school year, or all classes of teacher contracts (probationary, established, and professional) could be cancelled immediately for seven stated reasons.

2. The only "surviving" indefinite teacher contract language that was retained in 2011 appears at IC 20-28-6-8 in the established teacher category. This code pooled together the great majority of all teachers who had previously attained indefinite contract status (and added teachers hired for 2011-2012 and continued for 2012-2013), and gave them a continuing indefinite contract as long as they teach for the same school corporation.

C. Service under a Supplemental Service Teacher's Contract formerly counted toward achieving continuing indefinite contract status when the teacher served more than one hundred twenty (120) days in a school year. This is no longer the law due to the 2011 amendment, but it does permit these teachers to become established provided they taught at least 120 days on the Supplemental Contract before July 1, 2012 and then entered into a contract for further service before July 1, 2012. IC 20-28-6, sections 7 and 8.

Title IX 20 U.S.C. § 1681 *et seq.*, with regulations at 34 C.F.R. section 106.1 *et seq.* (See Chapter Nine in the main text.)

Points of Emphasis:

A. As applied to students, Title IX creates protection from discrimination based on gender in educational programs or activities in institutions receiving federal funds, including sexual harassment, athletics, and academics.

B. The Office for Civil Rights (OCR) of the U.S. Department of Education is the administrative agency empowered to enforce Title IX violations and it has the authority to ultimately deny federal funds to the recipient school district.

C. For the school to be liable for teacher to student sexual harassment violations under Title IX, school officials must have known of the occurrence and reacted with deliberate indifference. *Gebser v. Lago Vista Indep. Sch. Dist.*, 524 U.S. 274 (1998).

E. To be liable for student to student sexual harassment, school officials must not only have known and reacted with deliberate indifference, but the harassment must have been so severe, pervasive, and objectively offensive that it undermined and detracted from the victims' educational experience in such a way as to effectively deny them equal access to an institution's resources and opportunities. *Davis v. Monroe County Bd. of Ed.*, 525 U.S. 629 (1999).

TORT LIABILITY (See Chapter Two in the main text and IMMUNITY and NEGLIGENCE in this Article, above.)

Points of Emphasis:

A. A school board may defend any member of the school board or any employee of the school corporation in any suit arising out of his/ her duties for, or employment with, the school corporation, provided the school board determines by resolution that such action was taken in good faith; the school board may also hold the employee or board member harmless from the payment of damages provided the person's conduct was not the result of bad faith or malfeasance. IC 20-26-5-4(17).

B. Tort liability, as well as protection from liability, also pertains to parent and community volunteers who participate in school educational and other activities.

C. A school corporation may purchase insurance to cover the liability of itself and its employees and volunteers.

D. Plaintiffs seeking recovery against a school corporation and/ or school employees must file a notice of tort claim with the school corporation within one hundred eighty (180) days after the loss occurs; failure to do so prevents a tort action from being filed. IC 34-13-3-8.

TRANSPORTATION IC 20-26-5-4, IC 20-27, chapters 1 through 12; IC 20-50-3

Points of Emphasis:

A. A school board may, but is not required to, provide transportation for regular education students.

1. Children with disabilities must be provided such if it is contained in the student's individual education plan (IEP).

2. Transportation of homeless students is required by IC 20-27-12, regardless of whether a school provides general transportation services. The definition of "homeless" at IC 20-27-12-0.5 includes "a student who is awaiting placement in foster care," but is not one who is in foster care.

a. If a homeless student temporarily remains in the original school corporation, but in another school attendance area, the school corporation must transport the student to the same building that the student was attending when homelessness occurred.

b. If a homeless student is temporarily staying outside the boundaries of the original school corporation where homelessness originally occurred, the original school corporation and the "transitional" school corporation of the temporary stay must reach agreement on transporting the student back to the original school if the student elects to continue there.

(1) Both the responsibility for and the costs of the transportation must be agreed upon.

(2) If agreement cannot be reached, the responsibility becomes mutual and the costs must be equally apportioned between the two schools.

3. Transportation of students in foster care is governed by IC 20-50-3.

4. If a school generally provides transportation, it also must provide it to **nonpublic school students who live on the regular school routes**; however, they **may be dropped off at the point on the regular route that is nearest or most easily accessible to the nonpublic school**. IC 20-27-11-1. The Indiana Court of Appeals has ruled that such transportation is on a "space available" basis and the school corporation does not have to purchase or provide additional buses to accommodate nonpublic students when there is no longer seating for them. *Frame v. South Bend Community Sch. Corp.*, 480 N.E.2d 261 (Ind.App. 1985).

B. IC 20-27-9-1(b) prohibits a person from operating or permitting the operation "of a school bus on a highway in Indiana for a private purpose or a purpose other than transportation of eligible students to and from school," unless an exception is granted by numerous sections of said code.

Some of the exceptions contained in IC 20-27-9 are school-board approved transportation of (1) adults over age sixty five, (2) "eligible students and necessary adult chaperones **or of adults** to and from an activity that is sponsored, controlled, supervised, or participated in by the school board" (emphasis added), (3) pre-school students who attend the school, (4) special purpose bus use in certain listed situations, (5) a group or organization for any distance on buses operated under a fleet or transportation contracts, (6) persons with a developmental disability, (7) school employees to employee meetings, (8) use during a local, state, or national emergency, (9) agricultural workers under specific conditions, (10) children under age six to "day care centers' under stated conditions, and (11) the buses to and from a repair facility.

C. IC 20-27-8 applies to the standards and qualifications for the employment and contracting of school bus including being of good moral character, not using intoxicating liquor during school hours (nor to excess at any time), and not being addicted to any narcotic drug.

D. IC 20-27-5 establishes the requirements for the *employment* of school bus drivers (i.e., on a written contract), as well as the *bidding, awarding, and cancelling of transportation and fleet contracts* with the person or entity that is to provide the driver(s) and bus(es).

U-V

VACCINATIONS (See IMMUNIZATIONS and MEDICAL AND HEALTH RELATED in this Article, above.)

W-Z

WAIVERS IC 20-33-8-28 (See Chapter Six in the main text.)

Points of Emphasis:

A. Waivers come from two basic sources—first, a policy-maker (such as a school board, legislature, or a state agency like the State Board of Education can expressly authorize such) and, second, an individual (such as a school employee or a student and/or parent can voluntarily consent to be bound by a proposed governmental action).

1. Examples of policy-maker waivers include the State Superintendent of Public Instruction's delegated authority to waive school make-up days, a school board's ability to waive application of a zero-tolerance student discipline policy, or a school superintendent's statutorily delegated ability to waive all or a portion of the required three-semester expulsion of a student who possessed a firearm.

2. An individual, when faced with potential governmental action, is permitted by case law to waive the person's rights, **but only when voluntary consent** is expressly given and the person has **knowledge of the right that is being given up**.

a. In the school context, this most often occurs when an employee chooses to resign rather than be afforded the right to have a due-process termination hearing, when a student and/or parent decides to be expelled rather than through a due process hearing, or when a student consents to a proposed search of his/her person.

b. An often quoted U.S. Supreme Court case that thoroughly examined voluntary consent in a criminal context is *Schneckloth v. Bustamonte*, 412 U.S. 218 (1973), where the Court stated at 248-249 (bold added for emphasis):

> [T]he Fourth and Fourteenth Amendments require that it [the State] demonstrate that the consent was in fact voluntarily given, and **not the result of duress or coercion**, express or implied. **Voluntariness is a question of fact to be determined from all the circumstances, and while the subject's knowledge of a right to refuse is a factor to be taken into account, the prosecution is not required to demonstrate such knowledge as a prerequisite to establishing a voluntary consent.**

c. A Michigan federal district court ruled against a school for the strip search of a fourteen-year-old student and rejected the school's argument that the student consented to the search by responding to the allegation of hiding marijuana in his "butt crack" by merely saying, "I have nothing to hide." *Fewless ex rel. Fewless v. Board of Educ. of Wayland Union Schools*, 208 F.Supp.2d 806 (W.D.Mich. 2002). The court addressed the concept at 81 (bold added for emphasis):

> Voluntariness of a consent to a search should be determined from the totality of the circumstances, including both the characteristics of the searched party and the details of the interrogation... First, the Court should **examine the characteristics of the searched individual, including age, intelligence, and education; whether the individual understands the right to refuse to consent; and whether the individual understands his or her constitutional rights**... Second, the Court should **consider the details of any detention, including length and nature of detention, and the use of coercive or punishing conduct**... Further, the Court is to consider **indications of more subtle forms of coercion that might impact an individual's judgment**...

d. The Sixth Circuit has held that **there is a presumption against the waiver of constitutional rights.** *Tarter*, 742 F.2d at 980. When litigating the issue of consent, the **burden is on the defendants to demonstrate such a voluntary relinquishment of constitutional rights by the plaintiff**. *Id*. at 980. Consent must be proved by clear and positive testimony and must be unequivocal, specific, and intelligently given, uncontaminated by any duress and coercion....

e. The Indiana Court of Appeals has ruled that a teacher validly waived his right to the nonrenewal of his contract before the (former) May 1 statutory deadline when he requested and received an extension until May 20. *Thombleson v. Board of School Trustees of Cent. School Dist. of Greene County*, 492 N.E.2d 327, (Ind.App. 1986). The court stated at 333 (bold added for emphasis):

> Waiver has been defined as "the **intentional relinquishment of a known right**." *Lafayette Car Wash, Inc. v. Boes* (1972), 258 Ind. 498, 501, 282 N.E.2d 837, 839. *See also Salem Community School Corp. v. Richman* (1984), Ind.App., 406 N.E.2d 269. It is an election to forego some advantage that might otherwise have been insisted upon... **A person may waive a right created by statute if there is full knowledge of the existing right**. *Lavengood v. Lavengood* (1947), 225 Ind. 206, 73 N.E.2d 685; *Brown v. State* (1941), 219 Ind. 251, 37 N.E.2d 73.

B. The Indiana Student Due Process Code at IC 20-33-8-28 expressly permits a waiver of a student's statutory rights if certain conditions are met (bold added for emphasis):

> Any rights granted to a student or a student's parent by this chapter may be waived **only by a written instrument signed by both the student and the student's parent**. The waiver is **valid if made:**
> (1) **voluntarily; and**
> (2) **with the knowledge of the:**
>   (A) **procedures available** under this chapter; **and**
>   (B) **consequences of the waiver**.

CPSIA information can be obtained
at www.ICGtesting.com
Printed in the USA
FFOW03n1725270415
12931FF